KIDS & DRUGS

A HANDBOOK FOR PARENTS AND PROFESSIONALS

Joyce M. Tobias, R.N.

SECOND EDITION

Published by

PANDA PRESS

Annandale, Virginia 22003

First Edition - May, 1986; Reprinted October, 1987

Second Edition - August, 1989

 Published in the United States of America by PANDA PRESS
4111 Watkins Trail, Annandale, VA 22003

Library of Congress Cataloging-in-Publication Data

Tobias, Joyce M., 1937
Kids & drugs : a handbook for parents and professionals / Joyce M. Tobias. -- 2nd ed.
p. cm.
Includes bibliographical references.
ISBN 0-9616700-3-7 : $6.00
1. Teenagers--United States--Drug use. 2. Drug abuse--United States--Prevention. 3. Self-help groups--United States. 4. Parent and child--United States. I. Title. II. Title: Kids and drugs.
HV5824. Y68T57 1989
362.29' 0835--dc20 89-22789
CIP

A SPECIAL THANKS TO:

To my husband, Tom, who provided endless support, expert advice, the illustrations in the book, and the services of a mother and a father many, many times while I was submerged in this project.

To my seven children who have taught me so much, and who were so patient, understanding, self-sufficient, and supportive when I left their world and became engrossed in my own world of writing.

To all of my friends who contributed many hours of sharing, writing, editing, proofreading, and support.

To Phil Hickok who designed the front cover illustration and the PANDAA logo.

To the Junior League of Northern Virginia who financed the production and first printing of this book.

TABLE OF CONTENTS

INTRODUCTION

In 1980 a survey done in a middle class Cincinnati suburb reported that 38% of sixth graders and 89% of high school seniors said they used alcohol and/or drugs. However, only 38% of the parents thought their children used alcohol and only 8% thought their sons and daughters were using drugs.

I was one of the many parents in 1980 who erroneously believed that my children were not using alcohol and marijuana. My professional background as a registered nurse was no help. Two of my children were using alcohol and marijuana for a year and a half before I realized it. Their teachers and wrestling coach did not recognize their use. They maintained good grades and acceptable behavior at school despite the fact that they were often under the influence at school.

Our family life deteriorated as we tried to deal with our sons' chemical use. We were very fearful that our five other children would follow the example of their brothers. In desperation my husband, Tom, and I went to our school principal who assisted us in starting a parent group to tackle the problem at school and in our community. Through our involvement we found an excellent drug rehabilitation program. In treatment we discovered that all of the parents had experiences very similar to ours. Parents who were doctors, nurses, alcohol counselors, policemen, etc. had been conned by their drug-involved children for years. We learned that our sons' chemical use had had a tremendous negative impact on each member of our family. Each of us needed help. Our recoveries are ongoing. With the help of our Higher Power we chose to use a seemingly insurmountable problem to help us all to grow rather than to destroy our family. In gratitude we continue active involvement in the **War On Drugs**.

This book is based on my experience as a registered nurse, a parent of seven children, a foster mother to many chemically dependent children who went through treatment with our family, a volunteer in a treatment program, and as the founder of the parent group, PANDAA. Many parents and kids contributed information and personal stories to help others as they were helped. Through sharing ourselves and passing it on we find healing and recovery. All names in the stories have been changed.

The five chapters of this book include the evolution of today's drug culture; the progression of chemical use, its effects on the family, and treatment; the drugs of abuse; causes and prevention of use; and the formation of parent groups. There is also a resource section. Throughout this book, the terms chemicals, drugs, and chemical use refer to tobacco, alcohol and other mind-altering drugs. The term chemical dependency implies a dependency on alcohol and/or other drugs. ***This book is not for children.***

My hope is that this book will help families prevent chemical use or will lead them to recovery from chemical dependency; help professionals treat families and understand the enabling roles they can unknowingly play; and help citizens undertake action plans to decrease chemical use and availability in their communities. Because a need for the realization of the unmerciful impact chemical use has on non-users is a special concern to me, a young girl's story which clearly demonstrates this opens the book.

DRUG USE CLAIMS MANY VICTIMS

"Presently I am a junior in college in civil engineering, and plan to be commissioned in the army in a year. While I was growing up I lived in a family with two older brothers who were both chemically dependent on alcohol and drugs. From their example I never had any desire whatsoever to even try any drugs.

Both of my brothers were varsity lettermen and graduated from high school with at least a "B" average having taken higher level and/or advanced courses. To the outside world their credentials looked very good and no one believed they were doing anyone any harm.

In reality they caused large-scale destruction to our family. I never felt that it was safe to go home because my brothers' friends might be around. I spent as much time as possible away from home and joined as many organizations as possible in order to give myself, in a sense, a new family and people to be with. I became a sort of an introvert. No one could ever tell how I felt about anything. To the world I looked like a high achiever, I had very good grades and nine varsity letters, but I was and still am to some degree an emotional cripple.

Aside from my brothers who used drugs there were their friends and some of my neighbors. One neighbor in particular sexually abused me when I was ten years old and threatened me to tell no one, and I did not until about a year ago.

I was a totally innocent bystander and was hurt very badly. As a naive ten year old girl, then an endlessly terrified teenager, and finally a young adult I struggled to overcome all the feelings of inadequacy I thrust upon myself. For the past year I have been to a psychologist and now I am beginning to like myself. I am a person in my own right. All my life I had been told by the chemically dependent people around me that I was the cause of some if not all of their problems. My brothers' friends blamed me for losing my brothers' friendship when my brothers went into a treatment program and would no longer associate with them. They would throw me against the lockers at school and demand information that I did not even have, again "my fault," they said.

Probably the guy who raped me had the biggest effect on me. He had me totally convinced that he had attacked me because I was a bad person and worthless. But I was not the only one he attacked. Some of my friends in the neighborhood were also attacked. This was a sixteen or seventeen year old kid, who attacked us when he was either high or drunk.

I always felt so guilty about what had happened to me and constantly tried to prove I was a good person by excelling. My brothers and I were perfect examples of the "star" child but we were hiding our hurt. Just because you look like you have everything together does not mean anything. No one ever knew how much I suffered because I had it so well hidden.

If the dealers are not controlled, drugs are going to destroy our society. Everyone has the potential to be harmed directly or indirectly. Children are open targets for persuasion to use drugs or like me to be molested. We cannot protect them 24 hours a day. I have seen and lived in the problems caused by chemical dependency and never want to experience it again.

Drugs changed my brothers' lives, they were not the same people while they were using them. Now that they have been off of them they are different people. They suffered and know they hurt my family. Those years they were on drugs are years down the drain never to be retrieved. I now love my brothers again. It took a long time to forgive them for what they had caused me to go through. But I will never be able to forgive the people who supply the drugs and make it possible for people to get them without any trouble at all. Most of all I will not be able to forget all the pain and suffering that teen-age kid caused me even though I have not seen or heard anything of him since I was eleven. He went beyond the bounds of forgiveness."

This girl's family was totally unaware that she was laughing on the outside and crying on the inside. Within her family she was the perfect child and played the "hero" role described in Chapter 2 which many children of alcoholics and many brothers and sisters of drug users adopt as they are growing up. Her pain and secrets were brought to the surface through her involvement in the family oriented drug treatment program her brothers were enrolled in. Her ongoing attendance at Al-Anon meetings (described in Chapter 5 and the Resource Section) combined with professional therapy have brought healing and hope for a better adjusted adult life to this charming girl. As a victim of other people's drug use she has chosen to use her negative experiences as tools of growth. Fortunately she was exposed to the kind of help that enabled her to help herself.

THOUGH NO ONE CAN GO BACK AND MAKE A BRAND NEW START MY FRIEND, ANYONE CAN START FROM NOW AND MAKE A BRAND NEW END.

Carl Bard

1 TODAY'S DRUG CULTURE

Today, we are in the midst of a **Drug War** which has swept over our nation like a modern-day plague. A generation ago, illegal drug use was largely confined to a few groups. Now drug use directly or indirectly affects all ages and all segments of society - rich and poor - young and old. This situation did not arrive suddenly but has been developing over a number of years.

During the past 25 years, America's children have had the benefit of high quality nutrition, outstanding medical care, the best educational opportunities, and the greatest affluence in our country's history. Yet, during this time, the 15-to-24-year-olds has been the only age group with a rising death rate and an alarming increase in the incidence of suicide. While academic scores for grade schools were rising, high school SAT scores dropped during the 18 consecutive years from 1964 to 1982, and have risen only slightly since 1982. Nationally, our high schools are experiencing a 25% dropout rate. These disturbing facts are closely related to adolescent use of alcohol and other drugs. Adolescent chemical use has become so prevalent that an entire culture and life style has evolved around it. Knowledge and understanding of this drug culture can help adults to prevent and intervene in the devastating disease of adolescent chemical dependency. [1]

IT STARTED IN THE SIXTIES

Throughout history man has sought, used, and experienced the pleasures of mind-altering chemicals while also suffering the painful consequences of their abuse. In most cultures alcohol became the drug of choice and gained wide acceptance in adult society despite the detrimental effects of excessive consumption. But the use of other drugs such as marijuana and heroin were not tolerated by large segments of society. These drugs were associated with those perceived as lower class elements, jazz musicians or low-life characters. In the 1960's, the drug scene changed and shifted to the white middle class. College age kids linked the usage of so-called "soft" drugs, such as marijuana and LSD, to political ideology, revolution against materialism and quasi-religious experience. Although there were few scientific facts available on the effects of marijuana usage, it was promoted as a harmless substance, much safer than alcohol.

In 1965, the THC (the mind-altering chemical in marijuana) content was 0.1-0.2%. Young people used marijuana as a substitute for alcohol.

IT BECAME ACCEPTABLE IN THE SEVENTIES

Societal Changes: As the drug scene continued to evolve, other changes began to contribute to the further development of a new drug culture embraced by young people. Increased affluence and the baby boom resulted in record college enrollments. College dorms lifted curfews and visiting restrictions, and many became co-ed. Minimal supervision of large concentrations of young people on campus nurtured drug use. The Vietnam War became a volatile issue for young people and served to unite them into politically active groups which often confused civil rights issues with the right to "do drugs." Young people also argued that if they were old enough to go to war they were old enough to drink. Most states lowered their drinking age.

Marijuana was no longer used as a substitute for alcohol; the two drugs were often used simultaneously, and frequently with other drugs. Horticultural technology was applied to marijuana cultivation to increase potency. Between 1965 and 1970 the THC content rose to 1.0%, ten times stronger than earlier marijuana.

Pro-pot Organizations and Industries: In 1970, NORML (National Organization for the Reform of Marijuana Laws) was formed with it's primary goal being the legalization of marijuana. NORML and similar groups such as the Do It Now Foundation bombarded school systems and state agencies with inaccurate "soft on pot" literature, advocating so-called "responsible use." The sale of drug paraphernalia, pro-drug magazines, T-shirts, and jewelry became an overnight industry.

Drug Scene Extended into the High School Population: As the more potent marijuana moved down into the high school population, discipline and order in the high schools began to deteriorate. SAT scores went down. Dress codes were lifted. School smoking courts were opened and became hangouts for drug dealers. Affluence provided automobiles for students to leave school during the school day and "party" in empty homes. Vandalism increased. Bomb threats became so common that school systems wrote procedures for handling them. Nationally, dropout rates soared to 25%. Rebellious behavior became so commonplace that it was accepted as normal teenage behavior. Parents perplexed by their teenager's behavior were often told by professionals that such behavior was normal and that a little pot smoking was harmless.

In the late 1970's, sinsemilla, a new strain of marijuana stronger than hashish, appeared on the streets. The THC content was 3-6%.

By 1978, one in ten high school seniors was smoking pot on a **daily** basis. This figure doesn't include the groups most likely to be daily pot smokers, those who skipped school the day of the survey or those who had dropped out of school.

Keith . . . *"I did drugs at my junior high and high schools. By the ninth grade I was smoking pot at least three times a day during school. In addition to pot, I used pills, alcohol and LSD at school. While my friends and I were high we would burn things in the bathrooms and on the walls. At times we would break lights and lockers etc. I would say at least 30% of the kids were high during school. All my friends used to carry pipes, and bongs and rolling papers on their person or keep them in their locker. Some people I knew carried large quantities of drugs on them at school. They were the people who sold the drugs at school. In eighth grade just about every type of drug was available at school. Before drugs I had about a B average. By the eighth grade it was C's and D's. By the ninth grade I got straight F's. I also dropped out of all sports and extracurricular activities. Every part of school by this time was devoted to drugs for me. I got high on the bus and even in the classroom at times."*

Rock Music: Rock stars were open drug users both on and off stage. The lyrics of many rock songs were riddled with drug language, often times not obvious to parents (e.g. the Beatle's song, **L**-ucy in the **S**-ky with **D**-iamonds = LSD). Unknown to most parents, rock concerts became and still are the scenes of blatant drug use by the majority of concertgoers.

Carla . . . *"I think rock music is almost a central part of the drug culture. Most all young kids involved in drugs dream of becoming rock stars to win the worshiping admiration of the other drug users. Musicians do drugs on stage, talk about drugs in an encouraging air with the audience and sing about drugs. I would rate rock music as number two on my list of priorities as a druggie only after drugs. When I did drugs, I always wanted rock music which would give me more of a dreamy unrealistic feeling when I got high. I liked going to concerts because there was a free and wild, abandoned attitude there. I could get away with anything there like smoking pot in front of the police, buying acid in the halls, and buying beer under age. I liked the excitement and almost sinister, pulsating, earsplitting rock music, that seemed to wipe out any memory of rationality from my mind. I would say at the very least 95% are high at concerts."*

New Philosophy: "If it feels good, do it," became a new motto. TV advertisers persuaded audiences that we never need to feel anxiety, discomfort or pain. In the professional medical world, a new class of legal mind-altering drugs, the tranquilizers, entered the market and were aggressively promoted by their manufacturers. Doctors found they could relieve their patients' anxieties by prescribing these supposedly safe, non-addictive, legal, mind-altering drugs.

Using chemicals to feel better and to relax became very acceptable to large segments of our population. Unfortunately, time proved that all of the legal and illegal mind-altering drugs can cause dependencies.

Acceptance of Chemical Use: Symbols of the drug world entered many levels of society. Drug slang words such as "cool," "grass" and "wasted," were mainstreamed into everyday language. OPIUM perfume was an overnight success. Alcohol was advertised heavily on TV by professional athletes and other role models. The use of both alcohol and other drugs was glorified on TV shows and in the movies. Music with drug related lyrics became popular and drug paraphernalia was designed to appeal to younger children. Grade school children were wearing feathered clips in their hair which were actually roach clips (drug paraphernalia).

The Courts: Leniency in drug cases became the norm in our courts and continues to be in the 1980's. Selling drugs provides very high profits with little risk of serious consequences.

IT IS A CRISIS IN THE EIGHTIES

The 1980's have brought an even more potent marijuana (from 50 to 100 times stronger than in the 1960's). In 1985, the average THC content of marijuana climbed to 4% and it ranged from 6-14% for sinsemilla. Potency has stayed relatively stable since 1985.

Surveys show usage is prevalent in rural, suburban and urban communities. Polydrug use (use of more than one drug) has become the norm with alcohol and marijuana being the most frequently used drugs. A survey conducted by the **National 1-800-COCAINE Helpline** from July to September, 1985, found 89% of the youthful drug abusers who called reported using three or more drugs at the same time. **The Drug Enforcement Administration Annual Report** showed an 11% increase in cocaine use and a 15% rise in PCP and illegal amphetamines in 1984. In the **National Partnership for a Drug-Free America 1987 and 1988 Surveys** 43.4% of high school seniors reported they had used marijuana, and 15.2% had used cocaine during the past year. In Washington, D.C., emergency room cases involving cocaine rose 134% during 1988.

Chemical Use in School Related Activities: Athletics, bands and clubs became especially vulnerable to the spread of chemical use since the peer pressure intensifies in these closely knit groups.

Mark *. . . "I participated in football, wrestling and baseball as a druggie. I won the State championship in wrestling as a druggie. In baseball I would do drugs before practice and games. I got drunk at two games while I was playing in them."*

***Linda** . . . " I kept my drugs and paraphernalia in my purse and locker at school because I bought most of my drugs at school. I maintained a C average with a failing of a class here and there which I blamed on the teachers. I played soccer for a while when I was a druggie. A lot of times I got high before and after games. I got high at school sponsored activities, everything from sports to dances."*

***Dave** . . . "My grades were all F's except for a few D's once in a while so I could play sports. I played basketball when I was on drugs. I usually got high before and after practice, or games."*

Junior High and Grade Schools: Chemical use has filtered down to the junior high and grade school level. A 1988 survey done in the public school system of Fairfax County, Virginia showed that 28% of the intermediate students had used beer at the age of 11 or younger. The **PRIDE 1987-88 National Summary** reported that 34% of kids had used beer, 19.2% had used liquor, and 7.2% had tried marijuana by the age of 13. In the **National Partnership 1987 and 1988 Surveys,** 18% of 9-to-12-year-olds reported they had been offered drugs, 15% agreed its easy to get marijuana, 7% said it easy to get cocaine, and 13% have friends who use drugs.

***Tom** . . . "I started doing drugs when I was nine years old. I used drugs for five years, until my parents put me in a drug rehabilitation program. The drugs I used were pot, alcohol, hash, ups, downs, prescriptions, PCP, LSD, opium and I huffed gasoline and aerosols."*

The 1980's also brought a new, enticing alcoholic beverage, the wine cooler, which is especially attractive to the very young and to girls.

Already, the wine cooler industry is a multi-billion dollar business. These syrupy, sweet drinks are a mixture of fruit juices, sugar and low-grade wine often displayed next to soft drinks. Wine coolers are not perceived to be alcoholic drinks by many kids and adults. The fact is that a 12 ounce wine cooler contains from 4-7% alcohol, which is the same alcohol content as a 12 ounce can of beer.

APPROACHING THE NINETIES

As we leave the 1980's, we find our country in the depths of a cocaine epidemic which is intensified by the easy to use, easy to get, highly addictive crack form of cocaine. Latin America will produce twice as much cocaine in 1989 as it produced in the mid 1980's. Crack use has brought with it a rate of crime and violence previously unknown in our country. The lucrative profits of crack sales is entrapping many teenagers into the business of drug dealing with all of the dangers that accompany it.

Adult Drug Use: The National Partnership 1987 and 1988 Surveys showed that the worst abusers of drugs are the young adult group aged 18 to 35. Use is now equal among women and men. Children are learning drug use from their parents. The emotional effects of parental use on young children is so great that many states are passing laws requiring counselors in elementary schools for these troubled children. The statistics on alcohol and drug related spouse and child abuse are rising rapidly. A new form of child abuse is occurring in America, one in ten newborns has been exposed to illegal drugs taken by the mother during pregnancy. It will be more difficult to prevent adolescent use if adult use continues.

Let Us Not Ignore the Gateway Drugs: In the nineties we must be careful not to allow the focus on crack cocaine to distract us from the harmfulness and destructiveness of other abused substances, especially the two most popular and frequently used drugs, alcohol and marijuana. Although marijuana is illegal in our country, one third to one half of the marijuana that is confiscated is grown in our country. [4] The immense availability of alcohol and the easy domestic production of drugs such as marijuana, PCP, and methamphetamine cannot be overlooked as intensive efforts are made to curtail the importation of marijuana, cocaine and heroin.

THE ADOLESCENT DRUG CULTURE

Over the years, the patterns of drug use and its resultant adverse behavior have changed so much that even parents who used drugs in the sixties and seventies often fail to recognize chemical use by their own children. Frequently, parents do not associate chemical use with the new life style that the child has embraced. They are unaware that high potency marijuana combined with alcohol precipitates more deviant behaviors than they may remember experiencing themselves.

***John** . . . "Professionally I am associate professor of Chinese. While my son, age 15, and daughter, age 13, were doing drugs, I was unaware for a long time that this was their major problem, even though I myself had smoked quite a bit of marijuana about ten years ago in the early 1970's. Indeed, that was part of the problem. I assumed "pot" to be a relatively safe drug, even though, if I could have looked honestly at my own life back then, I would have seen - as I now do - the extent to which my decreasing energy and motivation at the time could be laid at the doorstep of this drug. Luckily, I had weaned myself away from it, and again, assumed a kid could do the same. I was wrong on this count as well. So even with my own experience I failed to recognize for a long time what was happening."*

The adolescent drug using world is an alluring and attractive culture with a number of subcultures such as punks, heavy metal types and satanists. It is a distant and distinct world which cannot be interpreted by our own memories and experiences as teenagers. This drug using world is difficult for the non-user to comprehend for it has its own customs, values, rules, language, dress and body language. Rebellious attitudes and unusual behavior prevail. Their music is not only saturated with drug-glorifying lyrics but also with rebellion, masochism, satanism, the occult and an obsession with death.

In recent years, more drug using adolescents are being drawn into the practice of satanism and the occult. Experts who investigate the crimes of satanists and treat victims of satanic crimes believe the prevalence of this elusive and secretive movement is unrecognized by the general public.

John *. . . "My son became increasingly hostile, volatile in his outburst of anger - punching big holes right through the wall - and then darkly withdrawing into his cave-like room, which was designed as a shrine to heavy-metal rock groups and the death-like imagery they projected. He was also clearly in great pain and loneliness, although this was covered over for me by his outward behavior. I was frightened both for him and of him. My daughter, in the sixth grade, was following in his footsteps, getting more and more hostile, carving names of rock groups into her hand with razors, wearing tons of make-up, and basically spitting in the face of our family."*

As these young people enter treatment for chemical dependency, they must not only stop using alcohol and other drugs but they must also go through a "re-acculturation." That is, they must re-learn the values, rules and behavior of the main culture. They have had no emotional growth during their chemical-using years. Achieving adult maturity without adolescent growth is difficult.

IS ADOLESCENT CHEMICAL USE OUTGROWN?

For a minority, adolescent chemical use is only a phase and they enter adulthood either as social drinkers or as non-drinkers who do not use other drugs. Another minority curtail their use of illegal drugs as they enter their 20's, but they continue to have serious problems in their lives due to alcohol abuse. **The National Partnership 1987 and 1988 Surveys** indicate that the majority of adolescent users increase their alcohol and other drug use after high school. Usage tends to peak in the late twenties. Many bring their use right into the workplace. In a survey of 500 callers to the **National 1-800-COCAINE Helpline**, 92% reported working under the influence of cocaine. These statistics demonstrate the importance of prevention and early intervention during the adolescent years.

THE GOOD NEWS!

The 1980's have brought a powerful new movement across the country, **The Parent Group Movement**. Parents have joined together to form an army to fight this **War On Drugs**. They are distributing literature that tells the truth about marijuana, alcohol and other mind-altering drugs in their schools and communities. They are lobbying for legislation. All 50 states have raised their drinking age to 21 and have enacted tougher drunk driving laws. Parents are court watching and using the statistics they gather to apply pressure on public officials. They are working with the police in their neighborhoods. They are placing kids in treatment. Parents will not allow the greed of the drug industry to destroy our country's greatest resource, its youth. They no longer have to be numb and helpless as the parents in the 1960's and 1970's were. Now there is proof that mind-altering drugs are harmful, and there is help available for those who have become chemically dependent.

The media industry is beginning to change their approach to drug use issues. **The Partnership for a Drug-Free America**, a volunteer, private sector coalition of media and advertising associations is attempting to ***unsell*** drugs. The Partnership is creating the television, radio, newspaper and magazine prevention advertisements that have appeared across the United States since April 1987.

The U.S. military has proven it can reduce drug use to a very low level through its programs of education, drug testing, enforcement of strong policies, intervention and treatment. The private sector is beginning to follow the lead of the military. In the Washington, D.C. Metropolitan Area the **Corporation Against Drug Abuse** is assisting small businesses in setting up policies, intervention programs and drug testing programs.

The U.S. Department of Education has started strong initiatives to assist school systems in becoming drug-free. Surveys are showing that drug use among adolescents is slowly decreasing as more children report they perceive drug use as being harmful. Early drug education does work. SAT scores are beginning to rise as adolescent marijuana use gradually declines.

The U.S. Congress has made the drug problem a priority issue by passing the Anti-Drug Abuse Act of 1988. Our national government is now making an all out effort to solve this problem. The Surgeon General has taken a strong stand against excessive alcohol consumption. We as citizens have a responsibility to support our government's efforts and to become a part of the solution.

REFERENCES FOR THIS CHAPTER: Nos. 1, 2, 3, 4, 5, 6, 7.

2 ADOLESCENT CHEMICAL USE

CHECK LIST FOR SIGNS AND SYMPTOMS

At Home the Child May .....

- ❑ avoid the family
- ❑ avoid eye contact with parents
- ❑ have mood swings
- ❑ argue over nothing
- ❑ disregard or break rules
- ❑ act rebellious and tell lies
- ❑ use bad language
- ❑ act secretive or paranoid
- ❑ be obsessed with loud rock music
- ❑ have red eyes and crave sweets
- ❑ sleep a lot or stay up very late
- ❑ sneak out at night or run away
- ❑ receive mysterious phone calls
- ❑ display declining morals
- ❑ get in trouble with the law
- ❑ attempt suicide

At School the Child May .....

- ❑ have poor concentration
- ❑ lack motivation
- ❑ have declining grades
- ❑ be labeled learning-disabled
- ❑ blame teachers for problems
- ❑ disrespect authority
- ❑ be familiar to the administration
- ❑ drop outside activities
- ❑ arrive late, disrupt, or skip classes
- ❑ cheat, steal or vandalize
- ❑ get in fights
- ❑ hang around the smoking courts

The Parents May .....

- ❑ find it difficult to communicate with their child
- ❑ dislike the child's appearance
- ❑ dislike the child's friends or not know the child's friends
- ❑ be afraid of the child or physically abused by the child
- ❑ notice money and/or valuables missing
- ❑ make excuses for bad behavior
- ❑ blame the school for the problems
- ❑ blame the child's friends and/or their parents for the problems
- ❑ blame their spouse for the problems
- ❑ feel the marriage is deteriorating
- ❑ dread coming home
- ❑ avoid being with the family
- ❑ find reasons to work late and on the weekend
- ❑ become overinvolved in outside activities
- ❑ use alcohol to forget problems
- ❑ feel powerless
- ❑ sometimes wonder if he/she loves the child or spouse

If several of these signs are occurring chemical use should be suspected.

DRUG PARAPHERNALIA AND OTHER SIGNS OF DRUG USE

Articles for Storage: Marijuana and other drugs are stored and distributed in small plastic bags, foil packets, small jars, or film canisters. A large quantity may indicate drug dealing.

Seeds and Stems: Marijuana must be cleaned of stem pieces and seeds before it is smoked. Marijuana seeds are dark, football-shaped and about the size of large bird seed. Stem pieces and seeds might be found in baggies, pockets or small containers. The seeds may be used to produce a homegrown supply. The high-potency sinsemilla strain of marijuana does not have seeds.

Nancy . . . "My daughter convinced me that the potted plants growing on her window sill were a school project. Feeling very proud of her new interest in science, I helped her keep them watered. Much later I found out I was watering her marijuana plants."

Because marijuana is difficult to light, a pile of burnt matches is suspicious. The marijuana ash is smaller, more fragile and whiter than tobacco ash. Marijuana smoke has a distinctive, somewhat sweet, smell.

Handrolled Cigarettes: Handrolled cigarettes may contain marijuana or may contain dried parsley, mint or marijuana sprayed with PCP. A handrolled marijuana cigarette (joint or reefer) has an irregular appearance and is usually twisted on either end. Handrolling requires rolling papers which are sold in small packets. Rolling machines can be as small as a pack of cigarettes.

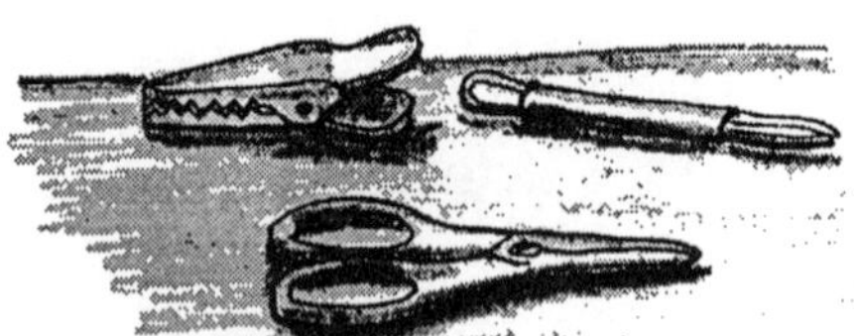

Roach Clips: Marijuana joints and other types of drug-treated cigarettes are smoked down to the butt (roach) and are often held by roach clips to avoid burning the fingers. Some clips are feathered or highly decorated.

Treated Cigarettes: Commercial tobacco cigarettes or marijuana joints are sometimes treated by spraying or applying a drop of PCP or a PCP substitute. Substitutes may include insecticides, such as RAID. There is no easily recognizable change in the appearance of the cigarette.

Marijuana/Hashish Pipes: Ordinary tobacco pipes are not suitable for marijuana, since it burns at a higher temperature than tobacco. Marijuana, hashish, and other drugs are smoked in pipes which are made of stone, wood, glass or metal. The pipes contain small, dime-sized screens which need periodic replacement. They are sometimes replenished with the screen from the kitchen faucet. Homemade versions of pipes are often made from empty toilet paper rolls covered with foil, soft drink cans, or from pieces of plumbing. Small probing tools are used to clean the sticky brown tar residue left from smoking. Some drugs can be smoked by burning them like incense in a partially covered container and inhaling the smoke.

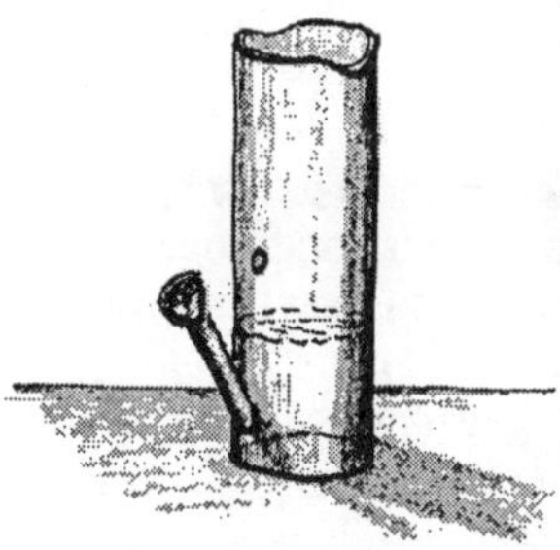

Bongs: A bong is a water pipe which is in the form of an upright cylinder. It is made of plastic or glass. A tube leading into the side of the cylinder holds the "bowl" in which the drug is burned. By sucking air at the top of the cylinder, smoke is drawn from the bowl through water in the bottom of the cylinder and inhaled. The bong cools and concentrates the smoke giving the user a higher dosage. The process of filling the bong with concentrated smoke and inhaling the smoke is usually called a "hit" or a "bong hit." A bong is often shared by a group since one filling of the bowl provides a number of hits. A bong can be used to smoke marijuana, hashish, PCP, and other drugs. As the 1986 federal law banning the manufacture and sale of drug paraphernalia is enforced, parents will be finding many more homemade versions of pipes and bongs.

Crack Cocaine Paraphernalia: Crack cocaine is smoked in glass pipes by vaporizing the crack. Vaporization of the crack is accomplished by applying heat to the pipe bowl with an ordinary butane cigarette lighter. Empty soft drink or beer cans can be altered to be a suitable smoking apparatus. Crack is also pulverized and sprinkled on a cigarette or joint. The presence of baking soda in a child's room could indicate processing of crack.

Snorting and Sniffing: Any powdered or pulverized drug, particularly cocaine, can be snorted. The drug is usually deposited on a mirror and shaped into a "line" with a razor blade or coffee stirrer. The "line" is snorted through a short straw, rolled dollar bill, or tiny spoon. Balloons and plastic or paper bags are used to sniff glue and other inhalants.

Intravenous (Shooting Up): Any drug which may be dissolved into solution may be injected. Supplies used are syringes, eye droppers, spoons for heating and dissolving powders, and cords or belts used for tourniquets.

Concealment of Usage: After depleting the home liquor supply, the user may dilute it with water. A taste test is in order when checking supplies. Soft drink containers often disguise alcohol. Girls hide small bottles of alcohol in their purses. Faked, forged, or stolen ID cards are used to buy alcohol. Breath sprays mask alcohol use and smoking. Incense, candles, or room deodorizers camouflage smoking odors in a room.

Hiding Places: Favorite hiding places for drugs include stereo speakers, trophies, lamp bases, books, albums, stuffed animals, air conditioner vents, parents' and child's out-of-season clothing, parents' rooms, car trunks, attics, garages, tool sheds and bushes. Commercially produced items for hiding the "stash" include weighted soft drink cans, hollow tape cartridges, fake Chapstick tubes, and many other ordinary looking items.

Hangouts: Shopping centers, especially stairways, hallways and game rooms; convenience stores and pizza parlors; school smoking courts; parks, beaches and secluded sites are common hangouts.

Suspicious Happenings: Bikes, clothes, stereos or other items may appear or disappear if they are being used in trade for drugs. School yearbook inscriptions often reflect changed values, as do posters, drug culture clothing, jewelry, record albums and magazines. Frequent short telephone calls, hanging up when parents answer, a caller refusing to identify self, prank and late calls are cause for suspicion.

Signs of Drug Dealing: Many users sell drugs to a greater or lesser degree. Signs of selling are a large supply of baggies, scales, unusual telephone activity, lists of telephone numbers, secretiveness, extra money, possessions that should not be affordable, expensive clothes and jewelry, heavy drug use with no apparent legitimate source of money, or refusal to allow parents in child's bedroom. Recently, beeper call transmitters, guns and weapons have become tools of the teenage drug dealer's trade.

PROGRESSION OF ADOLESCENT CHEMICAL USE

"Drugs cause addiction by controlling the behavior of users; that is, addicting drugs come to influence behavior leading to their own ingestion. Dependence-producing drugs can change the way a person thinks, feels, and behaves." [39, pg. 267, 270] The road to chemical dependency is gradual and subtle.

Chemical use almost always begins under the age of 20. The absence of serious physical consequences in the early stages affirms the user's belief that chemical use is safe and controllable. Chemical use is often described as having four stages of progression: experimentation, planned use, dependency , and finally, the burnout stage. In adolescents, the progression to a dependency state can take as little as six months or may take several years. The rate of progression depends on many factors: physical, mental, and emotional maturity, stress, boredom, family situation, peer group involvement, availability of drugs, types of drugs used and their route of administration, and frequency of use. Some will stop usage or stay in stage one or early stage two and maintain control of usage. When usage begins to cause problems in their lives, they are in late stage two and fast approaching the disease state. Alcohol use with no other drug use follows the same progression.

Stage One - Experimental Stage

Learning the Mood Swing: The user learns that the chemical makes one feel good. Few unpleasant effects occur. The chemicals most frequently involved are tobacco, inhalants, alcohol and marijuana. They may be given free. The child usually refuses participation several times, and often does not get intoxicated on the first alcohol encounter, or high the first several times marijuana is tried because the inhaling technique has not yet been learned. For peer acceptance, a high may be faked. In this early stage of use small amounts produce a high because no tolerance is built up. Drinking and doing drugs only occurs when it's convenient and available, mainly on weekend social events.

Behavior Changes: Acceptance by friends is increasingly important. There may be a change of friends, often older, or a long standing clique may stay intact and perhaps expand, as the group gravitates toward the drug culture. Rebellious attitudes towards parents and other authority figures, bad language, irresponsibility toward work and school, or a desire to develop a cool image may start before usage begins, during experimentation, or not until stage two.

Physical Signs: None are apparent.

The Parents: They are unaware of any usage unless they accidentally discover evidence or occasionally recognize the child is high or intoxicated. Usually such a discovery is considered a "normal phase" by the parent, or a strong, apparently successful disciplinary measure convinces the parent that the child has "learned his lesson."

Stage Two - Planned Use

Seeking the Mood Swing: Chemicals are bought and use is planned. Unpleasant effects occur as the high ends and a tolerance begins to develop (larger doses are needed to produce a high). New chemicals may be introduced such as hashish, hash oil, uppers and downers. This stage progresses from mainly weekend use ("weekend warrior"), to week night use, then daytime use, and possibly solitary use.

The Dual Life: A straight image is maintained in front of parents, teachers and straight friends while a totally different image is projected among drug-using friends. Druggie friends are often met away from home. Although drug use may be well hidden, the child puts an emotional distance between self and parents and other adults. Many kids are able to maintain a good appearance, good grades, athletic, and other extra-curricular activities for a surprisingly long period of time. ***The ability to lead a dual life also deceives the user into believing there is control of usage.***

At Home: As the child is drawn towards the drug culture, attitudes change and what was once unacceptable behavior is now cool and acceptable. Unexplainable mood swings begin, including withdrawal, anger and aggression. Verbal abuse towards parents, profanity and rebellious attitudes become a constant friction point between parent and child. Eye contact with parents and other authority figures is avoided. Isolation from the family is preferred and many hours are spent in the bedroom with loud rock music. The first signs of the amotivational syndrome (loss of motivation and drive) appear. Hobbies and extracurricular activities may be dropped. Everything is a "hassle," and all problems are blamed on other people.

Fran *. . . "I began to worry about my 14 year old when he became hostile, not just toward me, but to his sister. She had, up to now, been his best friend. I was bewildered by his urge to hurt those who loved him most. This puzzled me and I felt alone and wounded. When he ridiculed his best friend and abused other "friends" verbally I worried even more. Then other strange behavior began. He became insanely jealous of his sister and anyone he thought might get a crumb more of any treat he felt he deserved. He blew up at a moment's notice if he was asked to help around the house. He rarely talked, but when he did he revealed an alarming absence of reality in his thinking, planning a future career as an artist with no thought of education or of the marketability of his work. At home he was either arguing, complaining or locked alone in a bedroom, bathroom or basement.*

His moods swung from apathy to hatred. There was hardly ever any peaceful ground between."

At School: As grades drop, parents may react with strong disciplinary action. The child may bring up the grades, often by cheating or changing grades on the report card. The improvement cons the parents into believing the problem is improved or solved. Deviant behavior and use at school begins.

Runaways: Running away is a common rebellious and compulsive form of behavior which frequently starts during the second stage. Just the threat of running away can be an effective tool of manipulation. Suggestions for finding runaways are in the Resource Section.

Ruth *. . . "My 14 year old drug-using son, who had run away from home after an argument with us managed to stay away for days to my great surprise. Even though he carried no money or appropriate clothing, an entire network of druggie kids (and some enabling adults who were willing to believe his sad stories of abuse and unhappiness) provided him with food and shelter. I now know that before he entered the drug treatment program in which he is currently enrolled, my own home served as shelter for several runaways who spent nights in remote basement nooks, unbeknownst to the rest of the family."*

Morals: Vandalism, shoplifting, stealing, lying, and sexual promiscuity are common. As drug use and tolerance increase, stealing from parents and siblings may pay for drugs. Self-medication by getting high to relieve shame and guilt begins.

Physical Signs: Marijuana irritates the eyes, causing redness, which can be alleviated by eye drops or concealed by sunglasses. Marijuana may leave a sweet smokey smell like sweet hay in the hair or clothes. It can also cause stains and burns on lips, inside the mouth, finger tips or fingernails, and a craving for sweets. Dilated or constricted pupils, glassy eyes, poor muscle coordination, a runny nose, excessive thirst, bad breath, a weight gain or loss, change of appetite or a measles-like rash can indicate use of various drugs. Excessive tiredness is common because of the depressant action of the drugs and the late hour life style.

The Parents: Many parents enlist the help of school counselors, psychiatric social workers, family therapists, psychiatrists, etc., most of whom either completely fail to recognize chemical use or underestimate the amount of involvement and consider it a symptom of other problems. At this point, if the family is lucky enough to have chosen a professional trained to recognize adolescent chemical use he/she will refer the family to a drug rehabilitation program, because the child needs specialized treatment.

Stage Three - Dependency Stage

Daily and Solitary Use: Life centers on getting high. The child may advance to hallucinogens, cocaine or opium smoking. Drugs are used at school and on the job because distress is felt when not high. Drug use becomes not a choice but a necessity just to feel normal. Tolerance increases and attempts to reduce dosage or stop usage fail.

Feelings: The child is guilt ridden, depressed, feels paranoid, and self esteem is very low. Self-hatred sometimes leads to self-mutilation. Drugs are no longer fun. The appearance that drugs are still fun for druggie friends, makes the child feel "different." Rationalization of chemical use becomes an art. At this stage of use, depression is a likely diagnosis by a professional unfamiliar with chemical dependency.

Matt *. . . "I would steal money from my mother, go buy a lot of beer or pot, get real high, and after the partying I would come in early in the morning or not at all, and if she said anything to me I would curse her out or hit her. I would feel really ashamed and a lot of self hate, but I thought I was too much of a man to go and make amends and quit doing it. I thought I was a real man but I didn't even have the guts to admit I was wrong and I was destroying my family. I hated myself so much I would go out and beat myself in the face and scream and cry until I was too tired to do it anymore. Now, though, I am forgiving myself for the things I have done to my mother and to myself and to the rest of my family."*

Social Life: Family life deteriorates further. There may be physical abuse to family members and holes punched in the walls. Skipping school, sneaking out of bedroom windows (sometimes after coming home to meet curfew), running away, breaking the law, or losing jobs increase. Dropping out of school is likely. Drug use and paraphernalia are no longer concealed. This openness may be a way of asking for help.

Suicide Attempts: Suicidal thoughts occur and there may be suicide attempts which the parents may or may not be aware of. Danger signs of suicidal thoughts are suicide threats, statements revealing a desire to die, radical or sudden behavioral or personality changes, overt depression, making final arrangements by giving away possessions, making a will, or saying goodbye, and drawings or writings about death. A very depressed suicidal person may suddenly appear very happy because a "solution" has been found. Persons who have lost a close friend by suicide or who have already attempted suicide are at greater risk. Any expressed suicidal thoughts, danger signs, or attempts at suicide should be taken seriously. The child should not be left alone, any potentially lethal weapons or pills should be removed from the home, and the child should be seen by a professional and tested for drugs. [13]

Stewart *. . . "I felt depressed and hurt all the time. I hated myself for the way I hurt my parents and treated them so cruelly, and for the way I treated others. I hated myself the most, though, for the way I treated myself. I would take drugs until I overdosed, and fell further and further in school and work and relationships with others. I just didn't care anymore whether I lived or died. I stopped going to school altogether in the middle of my senior year. This was the most disappointing thing that I did because I knew how much potential I had and was willing to throw away. After this I quit my job and started not doing anything but sitting around at home and doing drugs in a vain attempt to feel better, or OK, or even normal again. All this was to no avail. I felt constantly depressed and began having thoughts of suicide, which scared me a lot! I didn't know where to turn, and I was too wrapped up in doing drugs and listening to my damned rock music to humble myself and admit I had a problem."*

The "Druggie Look": Some users will still look "straight and preppy." But more often the child may have a flat facial expression, ragged, worn clothes, "bop" walk (walk with a bounce), slouched stance and generally depressed appearance. Girls use heavy makeup, wear long bangs over the eyes, sexy clothes and jewelry. Both girls and boys strive to appear older.

Satanism: Signs of satanic cult involvement are a serious indicator of drug use. Adolescents in the dependency stage of drug use are especially vulnerable to the philosophy, physical and sexual abuse, crime, suicide and homicide promoted by satanists. In addition to drug related behavior, girls and boys may wear makeup to simulate death, earrings with peace signs, goat heads, or pentagrams (star inside of a circle), and dress in a punk style favoring black. They are often in a black mood, may talk of suicide, and some mutilate themselves. Heavy metal music with sexual and drug themes and black metal music with suicide and death themes are favored. Notes and stories written by these youngsters may talk of death and suicide, have cryptic symbols, or backwards writing. There are various occult symbols that may be manifested in clothes, jewelry, or drawings or left at scenes of vandalism or ritualistic activities. The most common ones are a pentagram, an inverted cross, peace symbol, anarchy sign (an A inside of a circle), the swastika (Nazi symbol), the death salute (sticking your tongue out), devil's salute (raising the index and baby finger), sign of the beast (three 6's), and a lightening bolt. Circles, goat heads and candles have deep meaning in the rituals.

Physical Changes: Overdoses, blackouts and flashbacks begin. There may be scars from self-mutilation. Chronic cough, facial puffiness, and frequent illnesses are common. Nasal sores from cocaine use may be present.

The Parents: At least one of the parents is often still in denial or believes the child is only using drugs occasionally. Marital relationships tend to deteriorate as the parents disagree on the solutions to their problems and blame themselves and each other for what is happening. Careers may go downhill because of preoccupation with family problems. One or both parents may begin to self-medicate with alcohol or prescription drugs.

Stage Four - Burnout

Chemicals Are Necessary to Feel Normal: Euphoria is rarely experienced from the drugs. Use is compulsive, uncontrollable, and continuous throughout the day. There may be "shooting up" (intravenous use) with cocaine, methamphetamine or narcotics.

Dean . . . "I really thought I had to keep doing everything everyone else was doing. That ranged from stealing cars, fighting, seducing the other guys' girls, all the way to major crime. Before I had a chance to wake up, I was picked up and my sentences totaled 17 years. It got worse. I moved to heroin, morphine, Demerol and Valium after I had already served seven years of my sentence."

Life Deteriorates: Delusions, paranoid and suicidal thoughts, overdose and blackouts occur frequently. The child is usually well known by the police. Physical health deteriorates. The user is often referred to as a burnout or a zombie. If treatment is not initiated, death will result from suicide, overdose, an accident, physical illness or other untoward behavior.

The Parents: They may separate, resort to heavy drinking or drug use, give up, or kick the child out of the house.

Chemical Dependency Is a Disease

Chemical use becomes the disease of chemical dependency when the user needs mind-altering chemicals on a periodic or continuous basis to feel good. The user is unable to control or stop usage, an increasing tolerance develops, and a psychological dependency develops which may be followed by physical dependence.

Tolerance: Larger doses are needed to become intoxicated or high.

Physical Dependency: The chemical becomes a part of the person's normal body chemistry and unpleasant physical symptoms, such as vomiting, tremors, sweating, muscle cramps, or even convulsions occur when the chemical is abruptly withdrawn. Acute physical withdrawal symptoms last for three to ten days, depending on the drug. Drugs that are fat soluble and that have a slow excretion rate like marijuana and PCP have less acute and milder withdrawal symptoms.

Psychological Dependency: A psychological dependency is much more difficult to overcome than a physical dependence because it lasts for the rest of the user's life. In other words, the user is never cured, but is always in either a recovering or active state of the disease. Hence, a user is never referred to as a "recovered" user, but a "recovering" user.

Characteristics: Chemical dependency is a primary, progressive and chronic disease which becomes a family disease as it progresses. Its cause is unknown although there is no longer any doubt that there are genetic tendencies for the disease in some families. [14] The undesirable behaviors associated with chemical use are caused by the chemical use rather than the chemical use being caused by other underlying factors such as inadequate parenting, learning disabilities, low self-esteem, etc. It progresses faster in women, adolescents and polydrug users (use multiple drugs). Dependency can develop in 6 to 12 months in some adolescents. Dependency on a drug seems to develop more rapidly when the drug is smoked or taken intravenously. No one intentionally becomes chemically dependent. Most studies show there is no preaddictive or prealcoholic personality. But, once the disease has begun, behavior patterns become very similar in all abusers. Fortunately, these personality changes are reversible if treatment occurs. Vernon Johnson, founder of the Johnson Institute and author of **"I'll Quit Tomorrow,"** believes that all abusers are guilt-ridden people with a very high set of values and morals which appear to be nonexistent because of their destructive and anti-social behavior resulting from their chemical abuse. [10]

Maintenance of Recovery: A recovering chemically dependent person cannot use any mind-altering chemicals. Even the small amounts of alcohol in cough syrups and other over-the-counter or prescription preparations can trigger a relapse in a recovering alcoholic. An alcoholic cannot use other mind-altering drugs, and a drug dependent person who did not use alcohol cannot begin to use alcohol. However, Dr. Robert DuPont advises in his book, "**Getting Tough on Gateway Drugs**," that with careful education of the recovering person, very careful monitoring by a well instructed family member, and a physician knowledgeable about chemical dependency, a recovering chemically dependent person may be able to safely use a tranquilizer, anti-depressant drug (Elavil, Tofranil, Sinequan, Lithium, etc.), or an anti-psychotic drug (Thorazine, Mellaril, Halcion), as part of a medically-supervised withdrawal procedure or to treat other mental illness. Dr. DuPont states that anti-depressant drugs and anti-psychotic drugs are not dependency-producing drugs. [2]

REFERENCES FOR "PROGRESSION OF CHEMICAL USE" SECTION:
Nos. 1, 2, 8, 9, 10, 11, 12, 13, 14, 39.

No one is easier to deceive than oneself.

EACH FAMILY MEMBER SUFFERS

As the alcohol or drug using person's behavior deteriorates, each family member experiences feelings of anger, shame, guilt, fear, hurt, loneliness and powerlessness. To relieve the pain of these feelings and to make attempts to cure the abuser, various defensive and survival behaviors are unconsciously developed by each family member. These responses may begin long before anyone in the family is aware that the problem is actually one of chemical abuse. Any of the following roles are likely to be adopted by family members whether the abuser is a parent or a child.

The Parent Enablers

Enabling Is Done with Good Intentions: Enabling protects a user from experiencing the consequences of use. It permits the user to continue alcohol and other drug use without being responsible for his own behavior. The enabler, in fact, assumes the responsibility for the user's feelings and actions. Most enabling is done out of care and love with the sincere belief that these helpful and compassionate actions will solve the problem. Unfortunately, enabling of the user only makes the problem worse by unwittingly allowing and even encouraging self-destructive behavior. If the user is an adult, the primary enabler will usually be the spouse; for the adolescent, the parents take on the role of the primary enablers. Other relatives, friends, school personnel, therapists, employers, co-workers, police, judges, etc. may also be enablers of the drug abuser. Their actions are very similar since they enable users by shielding them from accountability for their conduct. There are many enabling roles. Some of them are described below.

The Protector: This parent protects the user by rationalizing misbehavior; by bailing the child out of trouble at school, on the job, with the law, or even trouble with the other parent; by allowing a known user to drive a vehicle; by making special allowances that would never be given to the other children; or by keeping the problem secret from the spouse, extended family, and the world. Secret keeping is an important function of the protector and this nurtures and prolongs the disease.

***Marilyn** . . . "My daughter had trouble in school and couldn't graduate on time. I made a donation to the school and one year later she graduated. I sent her to college in Switzerland to get her out of the terrible environment in America. She did drugs all over Europe at the cost of $60,000. She was expelled after one year. I started eating compulsively and gained 100 pounds over the years. I started thinking that all of our troubles must be my husband's fault and that maybe if we got divorced everything would be fine. We had so many problems that I had a psychologist make house calls."*

The Fixer: The fixer tries to control things by taking on responsibilities that actually belong to the user. This parent may get the child up on time, call in false messages of illness, clean up the vomit from a drunken escapade, get a job for the user, or strike up bargains with the user. A common bargain is to accept usage as long it's done at home or in safe places.

The fixer will often attempt to fix the other problems rather than the chemical use. Some parents try to fix things geographically by changing schools or by moving to a new neighborhood. The fixer may look for special schools to help with the child's real or imagined learning disability. Special camps or programs may be sought to improve the child's low self-esteem, poor study habits, short attention span, or poor concentration. The child may, in fact, have problems which need expert, professional help, but these problems cannot be adequately treated when the child is also impaired by chemical use.

***Mary** . . . "We bargained with our son. If allowed to buy a Moped, our son promised to stay "clean." One week after he got his Moped, we found him with a baggie of marijuana, and he became so drunk at a party that the hostess gave him a ride home. That was when we both began to realize how powerless we were."*

The Peacemaker: The peacemaker minimizes problems, becomes a buddy to the user, and smooths over conflicts between the child and the other parent.

The Blamer: Both parents generally fall into the trap of blaming themselves, each other, the child's friends, the friends' parents, the school, the courts, and society. They may also blame learning disabilities, low self esteem, physical handicaps, or any other possible cause.

Denial That Any Problem Exists: Denial takes many forms. Chemical use by a family member can be too painful to accept and a parent may simply avoid the problem by denying its existence. A parent might avoid or withdraw from unpleasant situations by working late at the office, getting deeply involved in community affairs, or by self-medicating with alcohol or tranquilizers.

Parents May Alternate Roles: Both parents may switch doing various types of enabling.

***Mary** . . . "We took turns being hard and soft. In the past we had always been rather strict parents with a united front. Now we were belittling each others' solutions, as we each tried to solve crises in our own way. As time went on my deepest hurt was not from my chemically dependent sons but from the conflict that had developed between me and my husband. I never* *felt so alone. My self esteem as a parent vanished. It took a very long time for me to heal and regain trust in my husband, that together we could successfully raise our remaining children. That strength and recovery came through ongoing attendance at self-help support groups."*

The User Gains Control of the Family: As frequent conflicts continue, parents begin to believe that their declining marriage relationship is the cause of their problems. The physical health of one of the parents may deteriorate. Self-medication with alcohol or prescription drugs helps some parents cope. A parent's career may decline. The user becomes very skillful in exploiting this situation and becomes the controller of the family. The misbehaving user becomes the center of focus, attention, and energy for the family as one predicament follows another. Turmoil and chaos are the rule. Occasional quiet periods are only interludes between storms of family crisis.

Bringing the Second Parent Out of Denial: As one parent comes out of denial and recognizes that the problems are caused by alcohol or other drugs, the other parent may still be in denial. The parent who recognizes the problem first is usually the one who spends the most time with the child and handles most of the crises. The second parent may come partially out of denial, but may still deny the seriousness of the use, or insist that fixing the learning disability, fixing their marriage, changing schools, etc. will stop the drug usage. Progress is unlikely until both parents begin to come out of denial and are united in their approach. Sometimes denial is broken when the lead parent "lets go," forcing the parent in denial to experience firsthand the embarrassment, hurt, and anxiety caused by each crisis that occurs at school, at the police station, in the courtroom, or in the emergency room.

A greater understanding and awareness of unproductive and unhealthy coping mechanisms and their replacement by effective methods can be gained by attending self-help support group meetings such as Al-Anon, Families Anonymous, or Toughlove (See Chapter 5 and the Resource Section).

***Mary** . . . "My husband never denied the problem, but for a long time he believed he could fix it. Of course I ridiculed his solutions. I finally realized that I had to allow him to fix and fail, and to feel the pain of dealing with each crisis as I stepped back. Our son cooperated by creating crises more often. When our son could no longer manipulate us, he realized that he was powerless and became ready for treatment. Finally, we were all ready for the commitment that an intensive treatment program requires of the family."*

The enabling behaviors become just as compulsive as the user's chemical use. The enabler can become almost as disturbed as the user, and behaves nearly as irrationally as the chemically dependent person.

A Parent's Story of Recovery

"I am a recovering co-dependent. In recovery I have learned to talk about my feelings and would like to share my story. My goals in life were pretty much the same as every one else's in my generation - to grow up, get married, have children, and live happily ever after. I love children so I also wanted to become a teacher and be that perfect mom. Up until about 11 years ago, I thought I had it made - I grew up (physically anyway), became a teacher, got married and had four beautiful kids. Then something happened that wasn't supposed to happen. My second child began to have problems. What kind of problems? - drug problems. I sure didn't know what the problem was 11 years ago. But I knew one thing - MY kid wouldn't use drugs. Today, I know the word for that. It is called DENIAL! Denial is where many of us have been too long. I'm thankful I'm not in denial today!

Getting back to my son and his problems - (whatever they were) - SUPER MOM thought she knew just what to do - get counseling. Well, for seven long years we got counseling - family counseling, pastoral counseling, adolescent counseling, psychiatric counseling, and in-patient treatment in psychiatric hospitals. By this time my son had been labeled as being paranoid schizophrenic. I don't deny he wasn't paranoid, and there were times when he was out of touch with reality - but no one ever said it was drug-related. More and more prescription drugs were prescribed - added to his intake of street drugs. The entire family was getting sicker and sicker. The message I was getting from all this counseling and the message I was giving myself was: "I'm no-good - a no-good parent, a no-good person." I had lost all of my self respect. I was filled with self pity and resentments. I was immobilized with guilt, shame, fear, loneliness, hurt, frustration and completely helpless! They say recovery begins with misery. I sure had the miseries - 4 years ago my recovery began - a friend directed me to an alcoholism agency. Here I learned what the problem was - chemical dependency (a family trap) - a disease that affects every family member. At last I was in the right place. Through this agency I learned of other resources for people like me. There was a group called Concerned Parents, and there was Families Anonymous, a 12-step program for parents like me. There were couples communications groups. Oh, how great it was not to be alone anymore - no more isolation for me - people all around me to understand, to listen, to share, to care and to love me. Me, the person who had once felt so unlovable.

All of this involvement led me toward a complete change of life style (personality change). My children even accused me of having joined a cult. At least they were seeing a change! Change is scary for any of us. I would like to share some of what I learned about myself that aided in my recovery.

1. *I am a good parent - I didn't cause my son to use drugs - that was his choice. He did not choose to become chemically dependent.*

2. *I have learned to accept and forgive myself for not being perfect. I have made many mistakes - some honest, some not so honest. I was doing all the wrong things, for all the right reasons.*

3. *I don't need to cover up my true feelings with defensive behavior - my wants and my needs are just as important as anyone else's. I am important!*

4. *I needed to stop trying to control other people's life and learned to get control of my own life - give up my compulsive behavior (my addiction to my son) and to stop trying to be a fixer, protector, rescuer, manipulator - stop acting like a little god.*

5. *I learned how to practice tough love. What is tough love? To me tough love is loving my child enough to let him hurt for the consequences of his own behavior.*

6. *I know I have choices - I can choose how happy I want to be - I cannot change the things that happen around me, but I have the power to choose how I react to what happens.*

7. *I have established a new value system - one that is really mine. My behavior and my values had been in a great conflict. No more! I stand up for what I believe in. Inner peace - serenity is what we call it.*

8. *Most important of all - I have learned I don't have to go it alone. There is a power greater than myself - a spiritual power that is always constant, ever present - filled with grace.*

What was happening with my son through all of this? Oh, how I wish he were sitting here with me today. But it is not so. The reality is: not all people recover. My son went into an in-patient drug treatment program and our whole family became involved in a recovery program. To my knowledge my son never used drugs again. I'm grateful for the six months that followed that treatment. It was a time for us to share our love and caring and I was once again able to see him as a sensitive, talented, loving beautiful person. Obviously, he didn't see things the way I did. On an impulse (that compulsive behavior returned), he ended his life. You might say he recovered from his disease in his own way - certainly not the way I would have chosen for him or any other person.

When this tragedy occurred, I stumbled and fell - oh what a void in my life - one that I know will never be filled. Time helps - being able to share my story helps. But for the grace of God, I was able to stand up again and keep on walking. Through my recovery, I had regained my self respect, and put my false pride and false guilt behind me. I had love all around me - and hope ahead of me - hope for me and the rest of my family - and your families. Hope for a richer, fuller life than ever before. Let us all keep the word HOPE foremost in our minds when we are confronting this powerful problem we have with drugs, never underestimating our power as parents and professionals united!"

The Brothers and Sisters

Brothers and sisters get many confusing messages as they see their parents focus all of their energy and attention on the negative behavior of the user. Parents allow special privileges to the user and accept behavior from the user that they do not accept from the other children. Frequently, at least one of the siblings knows about the chemical use before the parents. Most often the parents are ***not told*** because of conflicting loyalties to the parents and to the using sibling. The user may also have threatened the sibling, or there may be admiration of the user. The siblings are guilt ridden from keeping the secret. Many have been physically abused by the user.

As the conflict between the user and parents continues, the other children in the family learn some enabling behaviors from their parents and participate in keeping family secrets. They also adopt various survival behaviors. These survival techniques inhibit the child's emotional growth and tend to be carried into adulthood. They also serve to enable the user. The same dynamics occur among the children if the user is a parent.

The Hero: The hero is too good to be true. The hero is an overachiever who is very responsible and gives the family a good name. The hero can be bossy, obnoxious, and achieves for approval or attention rather than for healthy motives. Later in life, these children are often workaholics, rescuers and enablers to their spouses and their own children. The hero usually leaves home early.

The Scapegoat: This child may be rebellious, irresponsible, disruptive and act out. The reward is negative attention, which takes the spotlight off the user. The scapegoat could easily be mistaken for a user and often use is in the future.

The Lost Child: The lost child is passive, apathetic, withdraws, shows little emotion, avoids conflict, does well in school but develops few social skills and may be overweight. On the surface the child appears to be calm and serene. In reality there is anger, pain, confusion and denial of the family's problem. Lost children have tendencies towards chemical use, compulsive eating, depression and suicide. As adults they tend to be loners.

Cindy *. . . "Before my brother got into drugs we were very close. When drugs came into our family, my whole family fought a lot. We got in physical fights often. But the main thing I remember about by brother and I was that we separated tremendously. He didn't want to have anything to do with me. I was terrified of him and didn't want to be left home alone with him. My brother would come home stoned and throw me around. Many times my parents weren't home to stop him. One time my brother did not like what I was doing so he shoved me across the room, I hit the dishwasher door and hit my back. I was really ashamed of my brother and didn't want my friends to even know I had a brother. I always held all my feelings in to myself. I would cry in my room by myself. I put off tough but I really hated what was happening. I closed off a lot so my parents and I had not really been able to communicate and a lot of their time went to my brother. At times I felt really left out. Since my brother has been in treatment, my family has changed a lot. We get along better. Since I also go to rap sessions, I've learned how to share my feelings and I've learned a lot too. I've got a brother back who is like he was when he was younger."*

The Family Clown: The clown gets attention by being funny and distracting and is often the youngest in the family. The humorous behavior covers up an inability to express feelings and pain. In adulthood there is a tendency to laugh away problems rather than to deal with them.

The Second User: It is not unusual when a child is placed into treatment to discover that other siblings are also doing drugs. Tragically, a second, third, or even occasionally a fourth sibling may also be using. In some cases the other siblings have witnessed devastating family misfortunes, even death, due to drug use, but still initiate usage or continue already established use. Some brothers and sisters are enticed to partake by the user to prevent tattling. The apparent popularity of the using sibling may attract another sibling to use. Others may want the same attention the misbehaving sibling is getting. Parents might have stronger denial about the additional users whom they thought of as their successes.

Each family member's defensive behavior becomes compulsive and habitual. As the family situation becomes too painful to bear, the person looks for a way out. If help is not found through self-help groups such as Al-Anon, Alateen or a family rehabilitation program, the person may use other forms of escape such as leaving the family, self medicating with alcohol or other drugs, or worst of all, suicide. With the proper help the chemically dependent family can become a nurturing family again, but, without help, the family situation and the life of each member is only likely to deteriorate.

A Sister's Story of Recovery

"I never want to live through that hell again.

I can remember the shock of walking down the main hall of my high school and seeing my brother standing in the smoking area with a cigarette hanging out of the corner of his mouth. The crowd of people that surrounded him were wearing pot-leaves on their jackets and headbands. I was frightened by their looks and the fact that my brother fit in so well. My brother - my hardworking, straight A, athletic brother! Things like this just don't happen to people like you and me.

I can remember being afraid to come home after school, knowing that my brother would be there. My conscience kept telling me, "Just sneak in quietly and maybe he won't even know you're home."

I can remember the indescribable pain of hearing my brother tell my mom again and again that he hated her. I'll never forget the helplessness in her face.

I can remember the shame that I felt when friends at school would tell me that my brother's hair was too long. I suppose my friends never knew how much humiliation I suffered as a result of their comments.

I can also remember the terror of not knowing when a car accident or an overdose was going to end my brother's life. The sound of an approaching ambulance would throw me into a panic, and I held my breath and prayed until I could no longer hear its siren.

It was at this time that my brother's drug use began to change my life, and I was completely unaware of it. I became bitter towards people in general, and I rejected my old friends. In addition to turning away from friends, I found myself unable to concentrate on studies, as my mind was consumed with thoughts about my drastic change in character. I became increasingly frustrated as I saw myself slacking-off in school, and I knew that I was no longer the person I used to be.

I can remember walking down the halls at school in the most stylish outfit I could find, hoping that changing my outward appearance would change the way I felt inside. When I decided that fashion wasn't enough, I began to drink at parties. I saw alcohol as the key to gaining acceptance from other people. Unfortunately, I wound up lowering my self-image all the more.

Within months, my brother's drug problem had dug its way into my own life, and I was desperate for help. It was at this time that my family decided to seek help for my brother at a drug treatment program. The changes that my brother underwent in this program saved his life... and mine as well.

As the sister of a recovering drug user who needed support, I too, was forced to rediscover the values of life. I was saddened when I realized how I had given up so much of what I believed in. I had lost my self-confidence and motivation. I was no longer willing to help others or undertake challenges for myself. More importantly, I had lost my overall appreciation for life.

In the winter of my 15th year, I decided to redirect my life. Gradually, by joining youth groups and extra-curricular activities, I returned to being the enthusiastic person I once was, only now I was much more sensitive to the problems of others. I became much happier with my life. Now I have fond memories too.

I can remember going on family picnics. I recall going to the movies with my best friend, and then spending hours with her just talking.

I can remember being at a college party while on a swimming recruit trip and proudly telling the host, "No thank-you, I don't drink."

I can remember hearing the voice of a drug-torn girl at the rehabilitation center where I help out, "Debbie, you've got to help me!" - and the tears filled my eyes as I realized that I would..."

REFERENCES FOR "EACH FAMILY MEMBER SUFFERS" SECTION: 1, 8, 11, 12, 15

> ***"Next to creating a life,***
> ***the greatest thing one can do is save a life."***
> **Abraham Lincoln**

INTERVENTION AND TREATMENT

The user's denial of a drug problem makes it unlikely that he will voluntarily seek help. It is a myth that the user must "hit bottom" before help can be utilized. The family can learn effective ways to identify the problem and to intervene. Intervention may prompt the user to want and accept help. If diagnosis and intervention occurs in the early stages of the disease, a family action plan with some professional assistance may be sufficient to initiate recovery. Parents have more avenues for intervention before the child becomes eighteen. Late interventions usually necessitate treatment of a more intensive nature. Early intervention and treatment are especially important in the prevention of chemical use by other family members.

Putting the Clues Together

Support Groups: Self-help support groups such as Al-Anon, Families Anonymous, or Toughlove described in Chapter 5 and in the Resource Section are very helpful resources. Through these groups parents can find help for themselves, help in identifying the true problem, and can talk confidentially with someone who has been there.

Put It in Writing: It is very helpful to begin a journal and to record the dates of all the behaviors, events, and physical evidence which have caused concern with either parent. Tape recordings or photos of some incidences can be extremely effective. Such record keeping reduces both exaggerating and minimizing of events, and helps both parents see their child's behavior more realistically. It can also help to bring the child out of denial when the time comes for confrontation or intervention.

The Most Significant Behavior Changes: Rebellious behavior, bad attitudes, disrespect for authority, and a decline in the family relationship are some of the most tell-tale indicators of alcohol and other drug use. These warrant further investigation.

Additional Telltale Signs: Room checks, monitoring of phone calls, and spot checks of school attendance may produce other evidence. Record the findings in the journal. Relating concerns and observations to the parents of the child's friends might bring more information. Alcohol or drugs do not have to be found nor does intoxication have to be seen to warrant drug testing or a professional evaluation. Users are experts at concealment. Determination of how many or which drugs the child is using is unnecessary. If only alcohol or only marijuana is causing such serious problems, the child needs help. A parent's best guide is probably his or her own "gut feeling" about the child.

Drug Testing: Drug testing might be done when there are school problems and behavioral signs of chemical use without physical evidence. A positive drug test may aid in bringing the user or a parent out of denial. Testing should be considered especially after suicide attempts. ***Drug testing should always be done in conjunction with a professional assessment.*** Too often a urine test is negative when there is actual drug use. Regular urine testing may also be part of a family action plan for a child still in the early stages of use. Alcohol use can be monitored at home with inexpensive saliva dip sticks (See Alco-Screen in the Resource Section, pg. 111).

All drugs can be detected in the urine. A urine test is usually preferable to a blood test because the drugs are detectable longer in the urine than in the blood. There is a separate charge for the testing of each drug. One should be specific about which drugs are to be screened. A test must usually be ordered by a physician, although some laboratories now provide the service directly to the public. Adulteration of the urine with bleach, blood (including menstrual blood), salt, soap, lemon juice or vinegar can cause negative results. To prevent any adulteration of the specimen, it should be collected with no advance warning in the presence of a parent of the same sex and must be safely stored. A specimen can be stored at room temperature for three days, refrigerated for a week, or frozen for several months. Collect a specimen as close as possible to the time of suspected use, such as the morning after a late night out. If the specimen is negative, testing should be repeated at a later date. Marijuana tests have a high rate of false negatives, a false-positive test is rare. A test will not be positive for a non-user who has been around a heavy pot smoker.

DRUG	**Approximate Detection Time**
Alcohol	12 - 24 hours
Amphetamines and Methamphetamine	2 - 4 days
Barbiturates	
Short-acting (Amytal, Nembutal, Seconal)	2 - 4 days
Long-acting (Phenobarbital)	up to 30 days
Benzodiazepines (Valium, Librium)	up to 30 days
Cannabinoids (Marijuana)	
Occasional use (1-2 times/week)	2 - 7 days
Chronic use	up to 30 days
Cocaine Metabolite	12 - 72 hours
Opiates (Codeine, Dilaudid, Heroin, Morphine)	2 - 4 days
Phencyclidine (PCP)	
Occasional use	2 - 7 days
Chronic use	up to 30 days

The above table is for testing with the gas chromatography/mass spectrometry method. Since detection times may vary widely from person to person, the time intervals listed in this table should be used only as general guidelines. Factors such as fluid intake, method and frequency of the drug's ingestion, the patient's physical condition, and the test method's sensitivity can all affect a drug's detection time in an individual. There is a test for LSD, but at this time it is not a reliable test.

The Rapid Eye Test: The eye may show signs of drug use when the rest of the body shows no detectable physiologic evidence of drug influence. The Rapid Eye Test (RET) is a simple one minute eye test that can indicate if a person is under the influence of alcohol or other drugs. It is especially useful in determining drug use during the first few hours after ingestion. Although the Rapid Eye Test (RET) has its limitations, a positive RET can be considered "reasonable suspicion" of drug use and gives the go ahead to proceed with urine or blood testing. It is a quick, simple, non-invasive test which can be done by properly trained non-medical personnel, coaches and parents. (See Resource Section, pg. 111.) [16]

Before Intervention

Dealing with the Shock: For a parent who has been totally perplexed by a child's behavior for months, and possibly years, the news of drug involvement can be devastating. Its discovery can bring on an overwhelming tidal wave of emotions such as terror, anger, guilt, panic, bewilderment, grief, confusion, helplessness, feelings of failure, isolation and powerlessness. A parent may be unable to even say it out loud. Even stoical parents may break down and cry for the first time in their adult lives. It can hit harder than a diagnosis of cancer because of the guilt and sense of failure the parent experiences. The loss of pride and realization that the parent no longer has control of the situation is degrading. Blaming self, spouse, school and society is an early reaction. A call to a hotline or a self-help group is a good first resource for verbalizing and getting feelings expressed. The parents should take care of their own needs first. There is no need to act impulsively and immediately confront the child.

John *. . . "I was frightened both for him and of him; and beyond that, furious with him, practically hating him at times. And I was unbearably guilty; I was sure he was doing drugs because I was his adoptive father and he sensed that I rejected him. I was so confused about my own feelings that I did not know at this point whether I did reject him or not. Psychiatrists, family therapists, and drug counselors reinforced my guilt by attributing his drug use to problems in my marriage, problems which were being worsened or actually caused by his drug use! This self-doubt, leading to self-hatred for being such a terrible father, was for me the worst aspect of the ordeal."*

Begin to Heal: Support group meetings are highly recommended. The unconditional acceptance and the opportunity to share feelings offered by these groups begins the healing process so that one can begin to approach the problem in a constructive manner. Guilt must be resolved. It was the child's choice to do drugs. Not many parents gave their child the first joint! If anger and resentments are dissipated to some degree, a confrontation with the child is likely to be more productive. Parents tend to take the child's behavior personally. A first response to the child is frequently, "How could you do this to me?" In the support group meetings the parent learns that the child is doing this to himself and is not trying to destroy the parent. Association with a support group gives parents the encouragement needed when it is time to do the difficult things that are necessary to help a chemically dependent person.

Fran *. . . "I overheard my son make a drug deal on the phone. My feelings of shock and hurt were almost disabling, but little by little I realized that his problem was too great for me. With luck and a lot of persistence I managed to convince my husband that our son's life was out of control. We put our son, by now a very depressed kid, in a drug rehab program."*

If One Parent Is Still in Denial: A successful intervention is improbable if one parent is still in denial or is not ready to intervene. The aware parent will have to learn how he/she is enabling the spouse's denial and proceed accordingly. Support group meetings are invaluable.

Parents' Use of Chemicals: Parents need to make a careful and honest evaluation of their own use of alcohol and mind-altering prescription and street drugs. If they are using any of these substances to cope or relieve emotional pain, they need their own personal treatment plan.

Get Educated: Before confronting the child or making any big decisions it is best to learn about the progression of chemical dependency, its effects on the family, and treatment. (See Reading List in Resource Section.) Try to determine child's stage of use. Parents almost always underestimate the amount and frequency of use. Devise a plan of action before confronting the child.

Intervention

Confrontation: Don't confront a child about alcohol and other drug use while the child is high or intoxicated, or when either parent or the child is already upset. Other children in the family may be helpful in the confrontation if they are well prepared and concerned. When confronting the child, the family members should give good reasons why they believe there is chemical use, relate how the user's behavior affects family members, display a united front, and be ready to implement a plan of action. Avoid blaming, accusing, lecturing, preaching and reasoning with the child. Make special efforts to show care. Don't lay a "guilt trip" on the child. Users are already guilt ridden people.

Don't be surprised if the child denies any use, claims any drugs or paraphernalia found belong to a friend, or admits to trying it just a few times. Admitting to occasional usage often relieves the parents and cons them into believing that "at least my child is honest." It cannot be stressed enough that the parent will only learn "the tip of the iceberg" since lying is a characteristic of the disease. If the child denies use, the family action plan described below or an evaluation at a treatment program is still warranted. At this point, parents ought to trust their own gut feelings more than their child.

If it is apparent that treatment is urgent, or running away is likely, it may be best to take the child to a treatment program for evaluation, rather than risking an unproductive confrontation at home.

Marilyn *. . . "My oldest daughter was expelled from school for being a "bag lady." I didn't know what this was and she said her boyfriend sold drugs in school and she only collected the money from the kids for these drugs. She swore she never took drugs, and I believed her."*

Children in Stage One or Early Stage Two: Very aware parents may discover usage in stage one or early stage two of usage. If so, it might be halted by a family action plan of strict rule enforcement, a complete break with alcohol and/or drug using friends, meaningful consequences for deviant behavior, close surveillance, close contact with school personnel, increased efforts at quality time and communication within the family, and random urine and saliva testing. For a family action plan to work the parents must be finished playing their enabling roles and be ready to support each other in each confrontation or crisis.

Alcohol, over-the-counter drugs, and prescription drugs should be disposed of, locked up, or stored at a neighbor's home. A user cannot be expected to handle the presence or the smell of alcohol early in recovery. It is best if alcohol is not used in the home during this period. If this part of the plan is difficult for a parent another self-evaluation is in order!

Forming a parent peer group (see Chapter 5) or participation in a support group will teach parents about enabling behaviors and give support in enforcing consequences for undesirable behaviors. The child may benefit from Alcoholics Anonymous (AA), Narcotics Anonymous (NA), or an outpatient rehabilitation program. Family therapy with a chemical dependency therapist can be very beneficial.

Moving or changing schools, a favorite first attempt for a cure, does not seem to work. Drugs are available in all neighborhoods and all schools, public and private. Plunged into a new environment, the easiest way a child with problems can make friends quickly is through drug use.

Andy . . . *"I went to two parochial high schools. During the last year and a half of school, I was skipping classes 2 or 3 times a week to drink at a local bar. I had a lot of free periods during the day and got high either right in or by school or in druggie friends' cars at least three or more times each day. I had two teachers who knew I was high in their class every day and chose not to deal with it. They ignored it even when my own druggie friends pointed out I was high. In my first high school, I was caught once and suspended, and the second time I was caught, I was expelled. At my second high school, I was caught by the assistant to the dean, who was into "acceptance" with the druggies, and he let me slide by. About 200 of the 800 kids were high at school sometime during the week. Before I dropped out of school, I had second honors with a B average. I cheated in some classes, as much as the difference between an A and an F."*

Professional Counseling: Before employing any type of counselor or family therapist, it should be determined that the therapist believes chemical dependency is a disease rather than a symptom of other problems, is specially trained in the field of chemical dependency, and does not believe in "recreational use" of alcohol or other drugs for adolescents, or use of mind-altering drugs other than alcohol for adults. Group therapy seems to be much more effective than individual therapy.

Children in Stage 3 or 4: If the action plan for stage 1 and early stage 2 does not bring about positive changes in attitudes, behavior, and school performance, the child is probably in stage 3 or 4. The parents can no longer "fix" the problem by themselves. Professional help is needed.

Andy . . . *"My mom was extremely aware of my drug and alcohol use, but nothing she did stopped me from using them. I liked school and school activities because I was able to freely use drugs to almost any extent without being caught."*

Dual Diagnosis: When alcohol and other drug use is present along with mental illness the term dual diagnosis is used. The existence or extent of a psychiatric disorder cannot be determined until the person is abstinent from alcohol and other drugs for two to four weeks.

Stumbling Blocks to Treatment: Many parents are very hesitant to consider treatment because they are afraid of violent reactions by the child, stigma attached to being in a drug rehab, or that too much school will be missed. Parents might ask themselves if they would withhold treatment for a diabetic child who is resisting life-sustaining insulin shots. A characteristic of chemical dependency is denial, therefore it is almost certain the user will not ask for help. The parents must take charge. Many users really want help but cannot verbalize it. When they arrive at a treatment program, and talk with counselors who can really relate honestly about the feelings experienced by a user, they feel much relief. When asked to try the program for a short time they frequently agree.

Mary *. . . "My son was in the last quarter of his senior year and still getting good grades. We were torn between getting him help before his 18th birthday or allowing him to graduate. It was the hardest decision we had ever made. We decided keeping him alive and getting him straight was the priority. He did not know he was going into treatment until he arrived at the program. Much to our surprise, he was relieved to be there, signed himself in, and gave us each a big hug when we left. We knew we had made the right decision."*

Planned Intervention: Some counselors or rehabilitation programs will assist the family with a "planned intervention." Family members and "significant others" (boss, good friend) attend counseling sessions. Here they learn about the disease, plan how family members will tell the user of their concern and relate how the user's life style has affected them. A professional leads the pre-planned intervention. The care and concern shown by loved ones gathered together prompts many to agree to treatment.

"Let Go" and Allow the User to "Bottom Out": If parents feel certain the child will not agree to treatment, or the child has refused treatment, strategies taught in the self-help support groups may make the user ready to receive help. Bottom will be reached sooner if all enabling behaviors are stopped, the user is forced to accept responsibility for his/her actions, and crises are *allowed* to occur. Drug use becomes a hassle hardly worth continuing.

Rules for those under eighteen might include no use of the car and no parental chauffeuring as long as usage continues. Jail can be an alternative to bail. The user can pay for lawyers. The criminal justice system is sometimes used to precipitate treatment. The user may have to leave home if other family members are endangered. For those over eighteen the bottom line is often no home and no financial support provided for school, living, or legal expenses by the parents while using chemicals. Some can make it on their own and will take longer to bottom out. It is very difficult and very painful for parents to stop enabling. Sometimes the only thing they can do is to "let go and let God" until the child asks for help.

Judy *. . . "My 22-year old brother didn't enroll into a rehab program until my parents gave him an ultimatum - either get help, or move out of the house. The ultimatum was not easy for my parents. But they were desperate. It wasn't until they gave him that ultimatum that he began to look at himself and question his ability to "move out for good." He had tried to move out several times. But he would always return home -*

penniless, repentant and hungry. My parents always took him back, of course. They were fearful about his inability to keep a job, or stay in school. But we were powerless to do anything for him. He had to somehow learn to help himself. We knew that much."

LETTING GO

LETTING GO does not mean to stop caring, it means to not take responsibility for someone else.

LETTING GO is not to be in the middle arranging, but to be on the sidelines, cheering.

LETTING GO is not to be protective, it's to permit another to face reality.

LETTING GO is not to deny, but to accept.

LETTING GO is not to nag, scold or argue, it is to search out my own shortcomings and correct them.

LETTING GO is not to criticize and regulate others, but to grow and live for the future.

LETTING GO is to fear less, and love more.

LETTING GO is not to adjust everything to my desires, but to take each day as it comes, and cherish myself in it.

LETTING GO is not to fix, but to be supportive.

LETTING GO is not to cut myself off from others, it's realizing I can't control others.

LETTING GO is not to enable others, it's to allow learning from natural consequences.

LETTING GO is to admit my own powerlessness, which means the outcome is not in my hands.

LETTING GO is not to try to change or blame others, but to make the most of myself.

LETTING GO is not to care for, but to care about.

Author unknown

Derek . . . *"I was arrested on four charges of grand larceny and was taken to jail. I had been living on the streets for several months after running away from a drug and alcohol rehab. I committed these crimes to support my drug habit, and even broke into my parents' home and stole silver, a rifle, gold watch, a pearl ring, and other things I would never have touched except for the effect of drugs on my body and mind. My parents pressed charges against me to get me off the streets and hopefully into treatment."*

Marilyn . . . *"My daughter's suicide attempt was a blessing in disguise. It led us to treatment."*

Treatment

Self-help groups or outpatient programs may be adequate for users who have already bottomed out and are personally motivated to get straight. Those who are not motivated to get straight, have been unsuccessful in an outpatient program, or obviously need a controlled environment and highly structured program, will need a more intensive treatment program. The program will bring the bottom to the user.

Since treatment involves big investments of time and finances which affect the whole family, it is wise to search very carefully for a suitable program, preferably when the family is not in crisis. To locate programs, call the city or county substance abuse or mental health agency, hospitals, schools, local hotlines, local parent groups, and refer to the yellow pages for alcohol and drug services. AA, NA, Al-Anon and Toughlove do not give referrals, but many people attending these meetings are happy to share their treatment experiences outside of the meetings. It is best to visit prospective programs and talk to people who have completed the program.

Cost is a major consideration when choosing a program. Cost can vary from $0 to $800 and more per week. Programs supported by public funds generally have a sliding fee scale. Insurance coverage varies greatly. There are some private programs which have unique arrangements providing long term care at low costs.

For those under eighteen, a program that specializes in adolescents and has an understanding of the unique culture that engulfs adolescent use is desirable. Individual therapy has not proved sufficient for the initial treatment of chemical dependency, although it can be effective after the client has been drug free for a period of time. Programs that provide a stronger focus on group therapy than individual therapy seem to be more successful. Effective drug rehabilitation programs are strict and demanding of the user and the family. The family members must be ready to commit themselves to a large time involvement and participate in treatment themselves.

Self-help Groups: Alcoholics Anonymous (AA), Narcotics Anonymous (NA) and other 12 step groups are free and very available in most communities. AA and NA advise 90 meetings in 90 days for the beginner followed by frequent attendance for continued support.

Outpatient Rehabilitation Programs: The most successful programs are based on the 12 steps of AA, provide group therapy more than twice a week, do carefully monitored urine screening, and involve the family in treatment. City or county substance abuse agencies often operate a program on a sliding fee scale.

Structured, Intensive Programs: These programs are usually residential and may be hospital-based or located in a separate facility. They are highly structured, provide a controlled environment, and intensive daily therapy. They may last from 30 to 90 days or may be as long as one to two years.

Use of Antabuse: Antabuse, or disulfiram, is a controversial medication often prescribed by private physicians and used in many treatment programs. After taking Antabuse, contact with alcohol (including the minute amounts used in cooking, cough syrup or shaving lotion) causes a violent reaction consisting of flushing, a severe headache, respiratory difficulty, nausea, severe vomiting, sweating, thirst, chest pain, weakness, dizziness, blurred vision and confusion. Antabuse only deters a person from impulse drinking, not from using other drugs. It may inhibit the alcoholic from assuming full responsibility for maintaining sobriety, increasing the chances of relapse. On the other hand, short term use of Antabuse may bring a period of sober, rational thinking that facilitates recovery. One must decide if the physical and emotional dangers of Antabuse outweigh its possible good effects. [17]

Chet *. . . "I was in three different mental hospitals and five different inpatient drug programs. I got and used prescription and street drugs in almost all of these. I guess the main difference in the program I am in now is that I am in a totally drug-free environment. I was forced to look at what my drug use was doing to me by peer pressure from people my own age in our group who had been through what I had been through. One thing that I think really helped me was a feeling of belonging and sensing a lot of care and tough love. Since I have been drug-free for six months I feel a lot better about myself as a person. I don't put myself down or write myself off as a screw-up or nothing person. I have really learned the importance of being responsible and that it has a lot of rewards such as being able to hold a job and save money, having my family relationship back and really caring about and loving my family now. I also have good strong friends that really care for me and that will be strong with me when I need it."*

Chuck *. . . "After my parents realized I was using drugs they sent me to doctors, psychiatrists, and then finally, to a psychiatric hospital. I was in that hospital for seven months. I got my first cocaine there from a staff person. A couple of days after I was discharged, I was using other drugs again. My parents tried to help me in any way they could, but with no success. I kept right on doing more and more drugs. Finally at the age of 19, I entered a drug rehabilitation program. I believe the reason I recovered at this program was because I was pressured by my peers to do good things for my life and not negative things. I had to share my past and feelings for specific incidents I had encountered while using drugs. Then I was able to deal with these feelings rather than suppressing them with drugs. The program was designed in levels so that each level helped me regain an area of my life I had lost - self, family, school, work, friends and* *the law. The program also helped me because it was totally drug-free. In the psychiatric hospital I was in I could get street drugs."*

Features of a Good Treatment Program

Chemical Dependency Is Considered a Disease: The program believes that the unacceptable behavior of the client is caused by the chemical use rather than by an underlying cause. The user must assume responsibility for his/her own actions rather than blaming others.

An Alcohol- and Drug-Free Life Style Is Promoted: Counselors are drug-free. "Recreational" or "responsible use" of alcohol or other drugs is not acceptable. Mind-altering prescription drugs are not part of the therapy. Not only alcohol and other drug use, but also the drug culture must be rejected.

Alcohol- and Drug-Free Environment: Prescription and street drugs within the program are not available. Clients, staff and visitors are monitored for street drugs. Parents must understand that only programs which are able to control the environment 24 hours a day can provide a totally drug-free environment. Outpatient programs often use urine testing as part of their monitoring program. In an outpatient program parents have a responsibility to provide a 24 hour structured, controlled, alcohol- and drug-free environment to the best of their ability.

Peer Counselors: Some of the counselors are recovering users who can relate from personal experience to the pain the client is going through and read through the "cons" of their clients.

The Evaluation and Intake Procedure: The use of peer counselors during the evaluation and intake procedure is especially crucial to prevent a missed diagnosis. Urine testing alone is not an adequate diagnostic procedure.

Treatment Tools: The time-proven 12 steps of AA are used. There is an emphasis on facing the past and dealing with it. To keep this disease of "frozen feelings" in remission the client learns how to express feelings, and use communication skills and problem solving tools in place of using drugs.

Daily Support and Aftercare Program: Daily support is advocated in the form of group counseling and/or AA meetings for at least three months. Aftercare continues on a frequent basis, often in the form of AA or NA meetings.

Family Involvement: Establishment of good family relationships is a major goal of the program. There is counseling and education for the total family including siblings. This may be in the form of Al-Anon and Ala-Teen meetings. The family members learn to recognize and to change the user's unacceptable behavior. If family members do not change, their ongoing enabling behaviors are apt to facilitate a relapse in the user.

Re-entry: The client must learn to maintain sobriety in a drug oriented society. After adequate progress in a structured, controlled, alcoho-l and drug-free environment, the client begins a gradual re-entry into society, learning to remain alcohol- and drug-free at home, school, job, and during leisure time. Therapy which may be in the form of AA or NA meetings continues during re-entry.

After Treatment

If treatment was effective, the child will exhibit considerable changes in attitudes and behavior. There will probably be a "honeymoon period" for the parents and child. The child is likely to be loving, talkative, and a joy to have around. Changes are less dramatic if the user was not highly motivated during the treatment program. In either case, the child will be extremely vulnerable to relapse. A parent cannot consider the problem solved. Recovery of both the child and the parents has barely begun. Maintenance of sobriety requires ongoing involvement in an aftercare program and daily attendance at AA/NA meetings by the child. The parents should attend support group meetings at least weekly. The child and parents still must deal with many feelings, fears, and issues.

Feelings and Issues the Child May Face: The child may still be experiencing some residual effects of the drugs. A drug-free state is not attained until the marijuana and other drugs are totally excreted from the body. This will take a minimum of 30 days, and may be longer for a heavy user.

Guilt is present before treatment, but it may be intensified after treatment as the child realizes what he has done to himself and the pain he caused his parents. Anger and resentments are probably not yet all resolved. The family may continue enabling behaviors.

There may be another family member using alcohol and/or other drugs. A child who is in early recovery cannot survive the sight or smell of alcohol, street drugs or prescription drugs. Fear of being offered alcohol and other drugs by family members or friends can be overpowering.

Isolation at school will be a problem. To stay straight the child cannot associate with old druggie friends. Straight kids will also be hesitant to befriend him. Some teachers will be uncomfortable communicating with him.

Because drugs are sold everywhere, going out in public, to a mall, or to a movie can be very scary for a long time.

The child may agree that he cannot handle drugs, but may still believe that he can handle alcohol. A totally different life style must be developed.

Feelings and Issues Parents May Face: The parents may feel they are walking on eggshells, hoping to avoid any arguments or crises. If so, they are likely to overindulge and enable the child. The absence of crises and arguments sometimes makes a parent feel empty and useless. (Crises can be an exciting addiction.)

They might believe the problem is solved and are ready to totally trust this wonderfully transformed child. Other parents will be justifiably reluctant to trust the child.

Each parent will still experience a lot of guilt, anger, resentment and blame. There will be a lot of pain as the child makes amends for past incidents that the parent knew nothing about. Making amends is imperative for recovery.

It is very difficult for some parents to accept the fact that to remain sober their child can never again drink alcohol.

Recovering Kids Need: Unconditional love, lots of hugs, strictly enforced rules, responsibilities, and chores are all a must. Praise and recognition for positive accomplishments are needed. Re-entry to school will be one of the most difficult tasks. Inquire if there are any support groups or teacher mentors in place at school. The family should be the major source of leisure time activities during early recovery. New sober friendships will be made at AA/NA meetings. The child needs to be confronted for any regression to old manipulative or rebellious behaviors. These behaviors will return before relapse to alcohol and other drug use occurs. The child does not need a lot of freedom. Driving privileges should be earned and dealt with very cautiously.

Recovering Parents Need: Parents need their own support group to help them work through their pain, forgive themselves, and receive needed awareness and encouragement to correct enabling behaviors. They need special time for themselves. No longer can they allow their lives to revolve totally around the child.

The Family Needs: The family needs to share feelings, joys, secrets and hurts with each other. They need to laugh and cry together. Kids and parents have to confront each other when enabling behaviors or negative attitudes start reappearing. Each family member must be accountable for his own actions. The family cannot allow themselves to forget the past or old problems will resurface. Some parents leave some reminders of the past, such as holes punched in the wall. With a lot of effort on everyone's part, and a lot of time, the family will heal and reap the rewards of working together as a unit.

A Psychiatrist's View on Marijuana

"In my experience there is only one certain way to be cured from marijuana smoking. The user must be totally isolated from the drug for a minimum of three months. Only after a period of sustained abstinence will the user become aware of the profound effects the drug has had on him and, at the same time, become free of its addictive effects.

The inability of the user to perceive himself or gain insight into what has happened to him over time is one of the truly pernicious and remarkable aspects of the effects of the drug. Talking rarely works; forthright decisive action by someone willing and able to take responsibility for the fate of the user is necessary. The chronic and heavy, and probably even moderate user, cannot take responsibility for himself.

How the person or persons exercise their responsibility to the user depends on the age of the user, his life circumstances, the severity of the retrogressive changes and deterioration of the user, and so on. I recommend sparing no effort whatsoever in achieving this objective. Searches are in order, use of police to back up parental authority if necessary, hiring a companion for the user, confinement to the home and hospitalization are all methods that I have recommended and have seen used.

Someone who cares must intervene, totally, consistently and with unrelenting perseverance. Efforts short of an all-out effort generally fail.

In summary, I believe chronic marijuana use affects judgment, motivation, perception, cognition and will. In addition, the drug causes an overall deterioration of personality; it leads to an estrangement from the mainstream of life; it lowers performance in all areas; and it leads to a social phenomenon in which users bond together into both loose and tightly bound subsocial groups. The effects on the user's family life is frequently devastating." [18]

By Harold M. Voth, M.D., Senior Psychiatrist and Psychoanalyst, The Menninger Foundation, Topeka, Kansas; Associate Chief of Psychiatry for Education, Topeka Veterans Administration Medical Center, Topeka, Kansas; Clinical Professor of Psychiatry, School of Medicine, University of Kansas, Kansas City, Kansas; Rear Admiral, Medical Corps, United States Naval Reserve. Reprinted with permission.

Our Son Is Getting Well

"We're one of the lucky ones. Ours is a success story. Our son will be graduating this fall, not from high school as we had hoped, but from a drug rehab program. We are filled with tremendous pride as we watch him reclaim his life, his values, his dreams and his future. For the past two years, we stood by essentially helpless as we watched him begin to lose his life to drugs, to deteriorate from a bright active teenager to a sad, unpredictable, often violent, drug dependent monster.

We sought professional help from psychiatrists, psychologists, school counselors and the church, but a child on drugs has an uncanny ability to con adults. Also, if he thinks he doesn't need help, he won't accept it. We felt guilty, frightened, angry, and especially out of control. The fact that he smoked pot and drank did not warrant the attention of the professionals as being "that serious."

A rehab program, when we faced it, was the only answer. After we got our son into such a program, we learned he had been a druggie for several years, not two. Although, we considered ourselves good parents, we were naive. We believed him when he said it was under control and made promises that he would quit. We blamed poor grades and low self esteem on learning disabilities. We cried when he dropped out of school. We did all the things we thought were right, except get him the right kind of help.

The program our son is involved in believes the main reasons kids get started on drugs is peer pressure, and they believe it is peer pressure that gets them off drugs. The program also feels the family must be involved in every way to help their child and themselves. For the first time in years these kids re-learn respect and how to live for both themselves and their families. They learn how to help other kids and to care.

Have you ever wondered at the strange and unpredictable actions of your child, especially a teenager? If your child's personality changes, if he becomes easily angered and bugged on confrontation, if he becomes overly nice, but evasive, or very direct and disarming, he may be on drugs. If he argues over the slightest thing, skips school, has failing grades, loses interest in sports, shuts himself in his room with his stereo, is late for curfew repeatedly, and avoids you, he may be on drugs. If he has red eyes, a constant cough, frequent stomach cramps, changes in his eating habits and hygiene, he may be on drugs. If he hangs around "just a bunch of kids," has frequent and short telephone calls at odd hours from friends you don't know, and refuses to abide by the house rules, watch out. If you notice the appropriation of household items, articles disappearing, money missing and the loss of new purchases, he may be buying drugs.

Don't accept "you can trust me," nicely said, or "get off my case," nastily said. Find out what's going on, no matter what it takes, and then if he is into anything at all get him to a drug rehab center at the first sign. Stop feeling guilt and shame. You didn't put the first joint in your child's mouth, but you can get involved and get the right kind of help immediately. Don't believe that your child can handle the problem, or that you can. He can't and you can't without help. It only gets worse with time.

Our son is registered in college, is working part time, has a car again and is headed in the right direction. Even more importantly, we like him. He likes himself and he loves and trusts us.

We have a co-equal responsibility to get drugs out of our schools and neighborhoods, but while we're doing that, let's not neglect to get the drugs out of our kids. Kids on drugs are sick kids and they need help. The use of marijuana and alcohol is a disease of the feelings that becomes chemical dependency. It is the source of the symptoms and not a symptom. It is on-going and non self-curable. It gets worse progressively, and frequent use of pot and alcohol leads to the use of other drugs.

It is worth whatever it takes to get help for a child on drugs, and it takes our willingness to admit a problem exists. Get confirmation if you suspect anything, and then take action by getting the child into a position where he can help himself. Get him to a qualified drug rehab program."

REFERENCES "INTERVENTION & TREATMENT" SECTION:
1, 2, 8, 9, 10, 12, 16, 17, 18.

The Serenity Prayer

God grant me the serenity
To accept the things I cannot change,
Courage to change the things I can,
And wisdom to know the difference.

3 MIND-ALTERING DRUGS

THE GATEWAY DRUGS

The four most widely used mind-altering drugs in America are nicotine, alcohol, marijuana and cocaine. They are frequently referred to as the **Gateway Drugs**, the entry to all other drug use. Previously, they were considered as "safe" or "soft" drugs. Nicotine, alcohol and marijuana are almost always the first drugs used and are the first drugs on which a person becomes dependent. If these drugs are never used, other drug use is highly unlikely. Although it is not generally one of the first drugs tried, cocaine is included as a gateway drug. Its false safe image has catapulted this extremely addictive drug to the second most frequently used illicit drug in our country. The **National 1-800-COCAINE Helpline** found that 93% of cocaine users used marijuana first and 75% of adults who have used marijuana, 100 times or more have also tried cocaine.

ALCOHOL

About 65% of Americans over 18 drink alcohol, and 26% of Americans from 12 to 17 years old are regular alcohol drinkers. Alcohol is used as a relaxant and is associated with social gatherings and "good times." A substantial number of users seek the relaxing effects of this drug, to self-medicate, to "forget" their troubles, and to ease the stress of living. Even though it is a legal, socially acceptable drug, it is the leading drug of abuse, is addictive for many people, and has many unhealthy side effects.

Rate of Absorption: The rate of alcohol absorption is affected by a drinker's body weight, amount and type of food in the stomach, the number of drinks and time span in which they are consumed, the drink's dilution, the type of mixer used, and other minor factors. Women, small people, and young people experience a quicker and more profound effect than large men. People who have just learned to use alcohol need less alcohol to experience a high than "seasoned" drinkers whose bodies have built up a tolerance to the drug. [2] [19]

The alcohol content in a 12 ounce can of beer is the same as that of a 5 ounce glass of wine, a 12 ounce bottle of wine cooler, or one and a half ounces of 80 proof liquor (an average mixed drink). It takes the human body one hour to burn up the alcohol in one drink. Neither coffee, long walks, nor cold showers will speed the excretion of alcohol from the system. [19]

Immediate Effects: Alcohol is a depressant, but, initially, as the alcohol level in the blood rises, it causes a drinker to feel stimulated and confident. Alcohol is directly absorbed into the bloodstream from the stomach and small intestine, which, if full, absorbs it more slowly than if empty. The blood carries alcohol to the brain, where it affects every level of the nervous system. The drinker's emotional state can also influence the effect alcohol will have, (e.g. may increase depression or increase euphoria). When the amount of alcohol in an individual's blood (blood alcohol content, or BAC) reaches 0.05%, thought, judgment, and restraint may become more lax. The person may feel free of many ordinary anxieties and inhibitions and more at ease socially. At 0.1%, the legal level of intoxication in most states, voluntary motor actions become perceptibly clumsy. The entire motor area of the brain and the area that tempers emotional behavior becomes depressed at 0.2%. The drinker staggers and may shout, weep, or be easily angered. At 0.3%, the person becomes confused and may be stuporous. Coma can occur at 0.4% and death due to respiratory failure at 0.5%. Death can occur from a BAC lower than 0.5% if tolerance is low, if other drugs or medications have been used, or if any other increased absorption factors are present. A protective response by the body to an overdose of alcohol is vomiting. [19]

Effects on Driving: Because of the many variable factors affecting the absorption rate, the BAC charts used to determine when it is safe for a drinker to drive are not reliable. At a BAC level of 0.05% reaction time, coordination, visual awareness, attention, judgment, and information processing are already impaired. Alcohol reduces a person's ability to judge distances, speed and angles. Its effects are especially dramatic on night vision and on peripheral and distance vision. Impairment of color perception sometimes makes the driver unable to distinguish red from green lights. Because of its uninhibiting effects, alcohol causes a tendency in drivers to take risks and feel overconfident in spite of adverse conditions. It also causes impaired reflexes, forgetfulness and sleepiness. Alcohol is responsible for 60% of driving fatalities. The National Safety Council advises that a person should wait one hour for every drink consumed before driving. [2] [19] [20]

Effects on Adolescents: Alcohol acts directly on the hypothalamus gland, the center for emotional development in the brain. In the adolescent, the hypothalamus is in a state of chemical imbalance and this results in the mood swings characteristic of adolescence. Some scientists believe that frequent ingestion of alcohol during adolescence can impair emotional development, cause permanent imbalance of the hypothalamus, and be a factor in the development of alcoholism. [23] Evidence exists that alcohol blocks the release of the growth hormone. [24]

Effects on Women: Women seem to have a greater susceptibility to modest and nonintoxicating amounts of alcohol, as well as to excessive consumption. They are especially prone to alcohol-caused liver damage. At this time, there is no explanation for the sex difference. [22]

Memory Impairment: Memory loss can occur in both social drinkers and in alcoholics after moderate intake of alcohol. Most drinkers are not aware of these partial memory losses. A "blackout" is total amnesia of a drinking spree and any events occurring during it, but with no loss of consciousness. It can occur with a rapid excessive alcohol intake. Blackouts are a symptom of alcoholism. [21]

Chronic Effects on Body Organs: Continued use of alcohol damages and eventually destroys brain cells. Alcohol is six times more damaging to nerve cells than to other cells in the body. From 50 to 70% of alcoholics entering treatment have some central nervous system impairment. Long term alcoholics may develop the Wernicke-Korsakoff syndrome (the alcohol amnesia syndrome). [21]

Alcohol is highly toxic to the liver and can cause hepatitis and "fatty liver." Both can develop into cirrhosis (degeneration of the liver). Alcoholic hepatitis is the most common cause of hepatitis in this country. It is the most frequently misdiagnosed and unrecognized form of hepatitis. It can occur in those classified as "social drinkers." Chronic liver disease and cirrhosis is the third leading disease-related cause of death in Americans aged 25 to 59. [22]

Alcoholism can be associated with pancreatitis, stomach ulcers, and cancers of the mouth, throat, larynx, stomach, intestines, liver, and pancreas. Many authorities feel that alcohol abuse is the most common cause of vitamin and mineral deficiencies in adult Americans. [2] [19] [21] [24]

Alcohol has a toxic effect on the heart muscle, causing an enlarged heart, heart palpitations and difficult breathing. Heart failure can be the end result. High blood pressure is common among alcoholics. [2] [19] [21] [24]

Many hormonal imbalances are also caused by alcohol, especially in the reproductive system. In males, alcohol use is closely associated with impotence and infertility. In women menstrual disturbances may occur. Alcohol use causes increased insulin secretion, resulting in diabetic-like symptoms in some people. [19] [21] [24]

Dependency and Withdrawal: Physical dependence can develop after three to five years of very heavy drinking, but more often requires 10 to 20 years of heavy drinking. A psychological dependence occurs long before there is a physical dependency. Some professionals use the 5-5-5 formula: a young adolescent may become psychologically dependent in 5-15 weeks, a middle adolescent in 5-15 months, and an adult in 5-15 years. Alcoholics sometimes experience a decrease in tolerance as their disease progresses.

This may be due to liver damage. Early physical withdrawal symptoms may occur six to eight hours after heavy drinking has stopped and include nausea, vomiting, irritability, tremors, sweating, and insomnia. A more advanced syndrome, delirium tremens (DT's), can occur two to four days after abrupt withdrawal. DT's may result in increased blood pressure, heart rate, and temperature; visual, auditory and tactile hallucinations (sensations of crawling insects); severe confusion; heavy tremors; and possible convulsions. Even with proper medical care DT's can be life threatening or fatal. [19] [21]

Cross Addiction: A person addicted to alcohol will have some degree of addiction to other depressants. If an alcoholic experiences withdrawal symptoms and is unable to obtain alcohol for relief, symptoms can be relieved by ingesting tranquilizers or sedatives. A recovering alcoholic who uses any depressant drugs can experience a relapse. [25]

Cross Tolerance: An alcoholic has the same tolerance level for other depressant drugs as for alcohol. Alcoholics require higher doses of anesthetics and larger doses of sedatives than the average person. [25]

Interaction with Other Drugs: Of the 100 most frequently prescribed drugs, more than half contain at least one ingredient known to react adversely with alcohol. The interaction of other drugs with alcohol may be classified as antagonistic, additive or supra-additive. The effectiveness of both drugs will be diminished when the interaction is antagonistic. Alcohol inhibits the action of stimulants, anticonvulsants and some antibiotics. If the effect is additive, the effects of the two drugs will be intensified. Antihistamines combined with alcohol will produce more sedation and impair driving skills more than if either drug were taken alone. Alcohol combined with marijuana results in poorer driving performance than when either substance is used alone. A California study of alcohol-related auto driver fatalities found that 81% also had THC in their blood. [31] A supra-additive interaction produces significantly stronger effects. A blood alcohol level as low as 0.1% combined with barbiturates can cause death. Tranquilizers, anesthetics, and narcotics, combined with alcohol have additive or supra-additive reactions. Because aspirin delays clotting time, it can cause massive bleeding in the stomach of an alcoholic who has gastritis. Heavy users of alcohol and Tylenol are particularly vulnerable to liver damage. To prevent undesirable interactions or reactions, read labels and check with your doctor or pharmacist. [19] [21]

REFERENCES FOR ALCOHOL: 2, 17, 19, 20, 21, 23, 24, 25, 31.

It's all right to drink like a fish,
if you drink what a fish drinks!

MARIJUANA

Description: Marijuana (Cannabis sativa) is a plant which contains 421 chemicals. The effects of most are unknown. Sixty-one of the chemicals are cannabinoids. In 1964 the principal intoxicating chemical in marijuana was identified as the cannabinoid, delta-9-tetrahydrocannabinol (THC). Improved plant genetics and cultivation techniques have dramatically increased the THC content of marijuana in recent years. Seizures made by the U.S. government in 1965 had an average THC content of 0.1-0.2%. In the late 1980's government seizures averaged 4% THC. The most potent strain, sinsemilla, has a THC content ranging from 6-14%. The potency of marijuana is now 40 to 100 times stronger than in 1965. From one third to one half of the marijuana seizures in the late 1980's were domestically grown. [4]

Derivatives: Hashish or "hash" is the resin extracted from the dried flowering top of the marijuana plant. It is compressed into brown or black cakes or balls. The THC content of hashish averages 3-4%. Hash oil is a concentrated syrupy liquid that varies in color from clear to black. Its average THC content is 14-21%. Thai sticks are marijuana buds bound onto short sections of bamboo, the average THC is 5.8%. Pure THC is never sold on the street because it is very unstable and too costly to manufacture. What is sometimes sold as THC is actually PCP or some other drug.

Slang Terms: Pot, grass, dope, Mary Jane, M.J., sens, reefer, weed, hemp, roach, and vegetable.

Appearance and Methods of Use: Marijuana looks like dried parsley mixed with stems and seeds. It has a sweet smell when smoked. It is usually bought in small plastic baggies, called nickle or dime bags. One ounce of marijuana will make from 40 to 50 joints (cigarettes). A joint sells for about a dollar, sinsemilla is much more expensive. Joints are hand rolled, smaller than tobacco cigarettes, and twisted on the ends. The butt end of a joint is called a roach and is often held with a "roach clip" and smoked. Marijuana is also smoked in pipes and bongs (described in Chapter 2). The marijuana ash is smaller, more fragile and whiter than tobacco ash. Hashish is smoked in pipes or bongs. Hash oil is dropped on a tobacco cigarette or a marijuana joint, or smoked in a special opium pipe. Dried marijuana is sometimes mixed in food but is only one third as potent when eaten.

Storage in the Body Cells: When marijuana is smoked or eaten, THC and the other 60 cannabinoids contained in it are absorbed by the lipid (fat) molecules present in every cell membrane in the body. ***"After smoking only one 3% marijuana joint, 40-50% of the THC remains in your cell***

membranes for four to eight days; 10-20% is still there at thirty days; and 1% to traces can be found from forty-eight days to 4.6 months." [30] The person is under the influence of marijuana during the time it remains in the body. The organs of the body that contain the most lipids and so absorb the most cannabinoids, are the brain, lungs, liver, kidneys, adrenal glands, ovaries, testicles and bone marrow. [30] THC has been found in the milk of mothers who have quit smoking marijuana three months before their babies were born.

Dependency and Withdrawal: Tolerance develops with prolonged use. Marijuana is psychologically addictive. Many authorities now believe it is physically addictive. Usually there are no dramatic physical withdrawal symptoms because of its slow metabolism and excretion. Physical withdrawal symptoms may include headaches, blackouts, nausea, vomiting and "panic attacks" (sweating, palpitations, heavy breathing and severe anxiety). [5]

Immediate Effects: Marijuana smoking cannot be compared to the social drinking of alcohol since intoxication always results from marijuana smoking. A single marijuana cigarette induces a "high" within minutes which lasts from 2 to 5 hours and usually does not result in a hangover. It gives an increased sense of well-being, and a dreamy, carefree state of relaxation. The user may experience sensations of floating and a more vivid sense of touch, sight, smell, taste, and sound. It can cause a craving for sweets and dryness in the mouth and throat. The pupils may dilate and the eyes may be irritated, red, or glassy. The state of intoxication may not be noticeable to an observer, even an experienced drug user. Marijuana suppresses the nausea center in the brain, enabling some users to consume large quantities of alcohol without vomiting, increasing the risk of death due to alcohol overdose. [1] [2] [5]

Effects on Driving Skills: In a study done in 1974 by Dr. Harry Klonoff, 38 drivers covered a 16 mile route from a university campus to the traffic-heavy downtown area and back again. They were rated by the system used to examine drivers for licensing. Final figures for the road test showed that those on the low dose (one joint with 1.2% THC) had a 42% decline in driving skills, while the high-dosage drivers (two joints with 1.2% THC) had a 63% decline. Unusual driving behavior included missing traffic lights or stop signs, poor handling of the vehicle in traffic, and unawareness of pedestrians and stationary vehicles. [26] A 1972 study of driving behavior in a safety-controlled area showed a "marked" decline in driving abilities was still present five to six hours after smoking, a "definite" effect eight to ten hours after smoking, and a lingering effect as long as 24 hours later. [27] It is important to note that today's pot has at least 4% THC. The **1982 Household Survey** by the National Institute on Drug Abuse (NIDA) reported that 60-80% of marijuana users questioned indicated that they sometimes drive while high on marijuana. [5] Marijuana metabolites have been found in more than a third of drivers in automotive accidents. [31]

Effects on the Body Cells: The cannabinoids' presence in the cell membranes inhibit the movement of chemicals and wastes in and out of the cell. The cannabinoids are not easily broken down or eliminated, consequently, they remain imbedded in the cell membrane for months. As more cannabinoids are absorbed, the cell membrane becomes saturated. Cell function is disrupted and the cells are robbed of energy, and growth and maturation of every cell system is retarded. Cell impairment is the most significant in the brain cells, the most specialized, most complex, and most fragile cells in the body. [30]

Effects on the Brain: In a study done on monkeys by Dr. Robert Heath of Tulane University, a heavy smoking group smoked three "monkey sized" joints with 2.5 to 3% THC per day, five days a week. A moderate smoking group, smoked one "monkey sized" joint twice a week. A light smoking group received one tenth the dose of the heavy smokers. A fourth group was given an equal dose of THC intravenously to control the variables of smoking effects. A control group was given inactive marijuana to smoke. The heavy, moderate, and intravenous groups showed lasting changes on their brain recordings after only three months of usage. The marijuana use was continued for an additional three months, and the abnormal changes persisted. Studies were done on their brains with an electron microscope eight months after marijuana use was discontinued. The heavy, moderate, and intravenous groups had changes in brain function and in brain structure which appeared to be permanent. Cellular changes were greatest in the areas which control emotion and memory. The findings correlate with the behavioral changes seen in marijuana users. [29]

Behavioral Effects: Two Philadelphia psychiatrists, Drs. Harold Kolansky and William T. Moore, conducted one of the earliest well-documented studies of the effects of cannabis on the psyche between 1965 and 1974 when THC content was 0.1-0.5%. Only patients who displayed no psychological problems or predisposition to mental illness before marijuana usage began were used. The only drug used by patients was marijuana and/or hashish. They smoked two or more times weekly, usually two or more joints each time. Common symptoms displayed included mental confusion, inability to concentrate, diminished attention span, loss of memory, loss of motivation, lack of goals, and declining academic performance. This group of effects is referred to as the "amotivational syndrome." Irritability and outbursts of aggression were common, especially if the patient was questioned about his personality change, new philosophy, drug use, or if his drug supply was threatened. Control of impulses and judgment were impaired. Most felt a growing sense of isolation from others, a desire to shun social activities, and deep-seated feelings of anxiety and depression. An altered sense of reality, and symptoms of paranoia were observed in many. All of these symptoms began with marijuana use and were reduced or disappeared within 3 to 24 months after marijuana use was stopped. [5] [28] A 1984 study done for the National Institute on Drug Abuse (NIDA) by Deadwyler explains how THC affects the hippocampus in the brain causing short term memory loss and the amotivational syndrome.

Effects on the Lungs: Marijuana burns at a higher temperature, and its smoke is inhaled deeper and held in the lungs four times longer than tobacco. Marijuana has 50% more cancer-causing materials than tobacco. Benzopyrene, a known cancer-causing agent, is 70% more abundant in marijuana smoke than in tobacco smoke. A "toke" of marijuana deposits four times more tar in the throat and lungs and increases the carbon monoxide levels in the blood four to five times more than a puff from a filter tipped-tobacco cigarette. [32] The irritants in the smoke of one marijuana joint cause about 20 times more narrowing of the air passageways than the smoke of one tobacco cigarette. More than 80% of pot smokers are also cigarette smokers. Heavy pot smoking can cause sore throats, bronchitis, sinusitis, pharyngitis, emphysema and other respiratory difficulties in a year or less. Marijuana smoke weakens the defenses of the lung against infection and disease. [2] [5] [28]

Effects on the Heart: During the "high," which can last from two to five hours, the heart rate increases from the normal 70-80 beats per minute to as much as 130-150 beats per minute. The blood pressure also increases. As a result, the heart muscle requires more oxygen. The marijuana smoke increases the amount of carbon monoxide in the blood, thereby reducing the amount of oxygen delivered to the wanting heart muscle, and weakening its pumping action. Only 10 puffs of a joint reduces by 50%, the amount of time one can exercise before chest pain occurs. These effects are particularly dangerous for the athlete. [5] [27]

Effects on the Reproductive System: Possible effects on the male include lowered sperm count, an increase of abnormal sperm, decreased testosterone (male hormone) levels, and breast enlargement. These effects seem to stop when usage is discontinued. The female may experience irregularities in the menstrual cycle, failure to ovulate, and lower female hormone levels. [2] [5]

Long Term Effects of Chronic Use: Unfortunately, enough time has not yet passed for good studies on the effects of long term use of the current high potency marijuana. Today's children are the experiment. Twenty years ago tobacco and alcohol had a much better reputation than they have at the present time. It would be surprising if the same will not be true for marijuana.

REFERENCES FOR MARIJUANA: 2, 4, 5, 26, 27, 28, 29, 30, 31, 32.

COCAINE AND OTHER STIMULANTS

Chemical agents which stimulate the central nervous system are called stimulants. Potent stimulants which have a high potential for dependency and tolerance are under regulatory control of the Controlled Substance Act. They include cocaine and the amphetamines. Two of the most prevalent legal stimulants are nicotine and caffeine.

Cocaine

Prevalence and Dependency Characteristics: Formerly thought to be non-addictive, cocaine is now often called the "Great Addicter." Users find the drug so pleasurable they may binge on it for days, staying awake and eating nothing during that time. In animal studies, it is the only drug that rats will self-administer until they die. A study by the **National 1-800-COCAINE Helpline** reported the average daily cocaine user calling the Helpline spent an average of $637 a week for cocaine, with a range of $100 to $3200. It is the fastest growing drug of abuse, and the second most frequently used illegal drug.

Appearance and Methods of Use: Cocaine is distributed as a white crystalline powder. The average dose is 20-100 mg. It is usually sniffed or "snorted" through a straw, rolled up dollar bill, or tiny "coke spoon", and takes about 3 minutes to reach the high. For faster, more intense, but shorter highs, intravenous injection will bring a high in 30 seconds and smoking in less than 10 seconds. Effects can last several hours, but the ***euphoric*** high lasts only 5 to 40 minutes depending on the avenue of administration. The high is followed by an intense crash or let-down, which the user often counteracts with another dose. The intravenous and smoking routes cause more rapid development of tolerance and dependence, and more harmful effects.

Slang Terms: Big C, blow, caine, coke, flake, nose candy, gold dust, snow, white and snow birds. Speedball is heroin combined with cocaine. [34]

Crack: Before crack, ether, a highly flammable and explosive chemical, was used to remove the impurities from cocaine to make it suitable for smoking (freebasing). The discovery of an easier and safer processing method using baking soda has brought the popular freebase (smokeable) form of cocaine called crack. The name is thought to be due to the crackling sound that occurs when it is smoked. It is ***perceived*** to be less expensive than other forms of cocaine because it is sold in small quantities. Crack looks like shavings or chips scraped from a bar of soap, or small chunks or rocks of rock salt. It is a creamy color, or light brown or beige, and packaged in small vials or tiny zip lock bags. The rocks are pulverized and sprinkled on a cigarette or marijuana joint, smoked in a glass crack pipe, or smoked in an altered soft drink can. Crack is five to ten times more addictive than other forms of cocaine. Use frequently occurs in binges lasting until either the user or his money is exhausted. Crack users tend to exhibit significantly more psychotic symptoms, suicidal thoughts and attempts, and thoughts or acts of violence to self and others than users of other forms of cocaine. Physical side effects are also more serious, especially on the respiratory, cardiovascular, and central nervous systems. [36] [37] [38]

Slang Terms for Crack: base, baseball, black rock, crank, freebase, gravel, rock, roxanne, snow toke, white tornado. Space basing or ghostbusters is crack doused with PCP. [34] [37]

Brand Names for Crack: Cloud Nine, Conan, Handball, Lido, Serpico, Super White, White Cloud. [34] [37]

Effects: Cocaine brings increased alertness and energy, talkativeness, euphoria, a feeling of being powerful and able to master any task, followed by irritability, anxiety, and apprehension. There may be enhanced sexual excitement and performance. Physical effects include dilated pupils, increased pulse rate and breathing rate, elevated blood pressure, increased body temperature, sweating, insomnia, loss of appetite, dry mouth, nausea, vomiting, abdominal pain and headache. Very high doses can produce tremors of the hands, arms, and legs, hallucinations, paranoia, disorientation and seizures. Traces of the drug in the body can be found for about a week.

Chronic Use: Chronic users are usually polydrug users, and rely on alcohol and/or other depressant drugs to relieve their tension, depression, and insomnia caused by cocaine. Relationships deteriorate, drive and ambition disappear, sexual desire and performance may diminish, and values change radically. Some will have auditory hallucinations, tactile hallucinations (imaginary insects crawling under their skin, often referred to as coke bugs), memory loss, blackouts, suicidal thoughts and paranoia. There may be bizarre, compulsive behavior, such as constantly cleaning the house, or feeling the need to defecate or urinate every few minutes. The user may totally withdraw and completely neglect personal hygiene.

Snorting cocaine constricts the blood vessels in the nose and causes a stuffy, running nose and nasal irritation which is relieved by nasal decongestant sprays. It can lead to nosebleeds, erosion, and even perforation of the nasal septum. Users may develop loss of energy, sore throat, damage to vocal chords, visual disturbances, headaches, sinus problems, weight loss, and trouble with their teeth, gums, nails, and hair. They may constantly lick their lips and grind their teeth, and have muscle twitches. Women may experience an increase in blood levels of prolactin. [32] Damage to the liver, heart, lungs and brain can occur.

Intravenous use of cocaine leaves the user vulnerable to blood infections, AIDS, hepatitis, lung abscesses and endocarditis. Intravenous cocaine use is quickly becoming a leading avenue of contracting AIDS.

Withdrawal: Immediate withdrawal symptoms, which may last for several days, can include profound depression, apathy, fatigue, and disturbed sleep for up to 20 hours a day. Anxiety, tension, impaired perception and thought processes, and suicidal tendencies may persist for weeks or months.

Overdose: Death can occur from convulsions, heart and lung failure, strokes, or asphyxiation. Death can transpire even when cocaine is snorted. There is evidence that sensitivity to cocaine may be enhanced by alcohol. [32]

Adolescent Use: One in five high school seniors has used cocaine at least once. [7] Dr. Mark Gold, founder of the **1-800-COCAINE Helpline,** reported in the British Medical Journal, **Lancet,** on a survey of 100 randomly picked adolescent cocaine users who called the **National 1-800-COCAINE Helpline** number. The number of 13-19 year old callers to the Helpline rose from 9% in 1983 to 17% in 1984. The typical adolescent cocaine user has a middle-class background, is 16 years old and a high-school junior. Although their parents did not approve of adolescent use, 44% said their parents used marijuana or other drugs. Most of the adolescents used other drugs to counteract the unpleasant side effects of cocaine: 92% used marijuana, 85% alcohol, 64% sedative hypnotics, and 4% heroin. In adolescents, cocaine use seems to lead to more rapid and more severe drug-related consequences than it does in adults:

69% were having trouble staying in school
44% sold drugs to support their habit
31% had been expelled from school
31% had stolen from friends or families
27% were violent
19% had suffered brain seizures
14% had or were attempting suicide
13% had auto accidents

Synthetic Cocaine: Synthetic cocaine is composed of a "caine" drug such as lidocaine or procaine and may contain ephedrine and phenyl-propanolamine. It is being sold legally as an incense in stores, and by mail order houses under such names as Toot, Florida Snow, Supercaine, Ultra-caine, Base-O-Caine, and Superior Caine. Deaths have been reported from these preparations.

REFERENCES FOR COCAINE: 2, 7, 32, 33, 34, 35, 36, 37, 38.

Amphetamines

Amphetamines are used medically for weight reduction, hyperactive behavior in children, and for narcolepsy (uncontrollable desire for sleep). Vast quantities are produced illegally for the illicit market and distributed by motorcycle gangs. Amphetamines are similar to cocaine in all respects except that they are slower acting with longer effects. They may also cause a measles-like rash. They are usually taken orally but can be snorted or injected intravenously. An experienced intravenous cocaine user cannot tell the difference between an intravenous dose of amphetamines and an intravenous dose of cocaine. [2] Some brand names are Benzedrine, Biphetamine, and Dexedrine. Look-alike pills are frequently sold as amphetamines.

Slang Terms: Speed, uppers, ups, beans, bennies, black beauties, bumblebees, hearts, pep pills, co-pilots, and footballs.

Methamphetamine: Methamphetamine is the most potent amphetamine. Legally it is used for weight reduction under the name Desoxyn. On the street it is sold in the form of white or brownish chunky powder or a "rock," which resembles a block of paraffin in appearance, but not consistency. Users shave powder off this rock and inject or snort it. This "poor man's cocaine" is expensive and very addictive. It is increasingly being injected for its powerful crack-like jolt to the brain.

Slang Terms: Crystal meth, crystal methedrine, crank, meth, speed. Poor man's speedball is methamphetamine and heroin.

Other Stimulants: Ritalin and Cylert used medically for hyperactive children, and the appetite suppressants such as Preludin, Didrex, Pre-State, Voranil, Tenuate, Tepanil, Pondimin, Sanorex, Plegine and Ionamin may be used abusively.

Overdoses: Symptoms may include dizziness, tremors, an agitated state, headache, flushed skin, chest pains, sweating, vomiting and cramps, high fever and possible convulsions. Fatalities have been reported among athletes who have been under extreme exertion after using moderate doses of stimulants.

REFERENCES FOR AMPHETAMINES: 1, 2, 33, 34.

Nicotine

Nicotine is a very addictive and poisonous drug. If all the nicotine in one pack of cigarettes were injected, it would kill an adult within minutes. *"The use of alcohol only progresses to dependence (alcoholism) in 10-15% of all drinkers. Use of cigarettes, by contrast, almost inevitably escalates to a level characterized as dependent use."* [39, pg. 262] Nicotine is found in tobacco which is either smoked, sniffed, or chewed. Smokeless tobacco is just as addictive and harmful as tobacco that is smoked. The blood nicotine level is higher among smokeless tobacco users than among smokers. [40]

Immediate Effects: Nicotine causes a release of adrenaline which produces a rise in the blood pressure and heartbeat. Sugar is released into the bloodstream and, along with oxygen, is rushed to the brain. This results in a definite high. The effects last for 20 to 30 minutes. Another cigarette is then needed to avoid withdrawal symptoms.

Long Term Effects: Excessive smoking tends to result in chronic indigestion, muscular tremor and general irritability. Nicotine's vasoconstrictor properties cause decreased blood flow to the brain, heart, and all systems of the body, making cigarette smoking a factor in poor wound healing, stomach ulcers, and many diseases associated with poor circulation. Cigarette smoking is the major cause of chronic obstructive lung disease. Because nicotine stimulates the release of adrenalin, the hormone secreted to handle emergencies, the "fight or flight response" is always in motion. This causes stress on the heart, making it work harder and require more oxygen. For tobacco smokers the decrease in oxygen caused by the carbon monoxide of cigarette smoke further taxes the heart's need for more oxygen. Coronary heart disease is the greatest cause of death in cigarette smokers. In 1975, 25% of such deaths were attributed directly to smoking. In women, tobacco smoking can be associated with early menopause and osteoporosis.

The American Cancer Society attributes one in five cancer deaths to cigarette smoking. Smoking can be related to cancer of the respiratory tract, upper digestive tract, pancreas, kidney, bladder and cervix of the uterus. The levels of N-nitrosonornicotine (causes cancers of the esophagus, nasal cavity, windpipe and lung in laboratory animals) are eight times greater in snuff and chewing tobacco than in cigarette smoke. [40]

REFERENCES FOR NICOTINE: 39, 40, 41.

Caffeine

Caffeine is a relatively mild stimulant if used in moderate amounts. One cup of coffee contains 85-100 mg. of caffeine. One cup of tea, and some soft drinks, such as colas contain about half as much. A one ounce chocolate bar contains about 25 mg. Some non-prescription drugs also contain caffeine: stimulants such as Nodoz; preparations for menstrual pain such as Midol and Aqua-ban; and analgesics such as Anacin, Cope, Excedrin, Empirin Compound, and Darvon Compound. In cold preparations such as Triaminicin and Coryban-D, it combats the drowsiness caused by the antihistamine in the cold preparation. Many parents are not aware that caffeine ingested by their children through soft drinks, chocolate, and over-the-counter medications is sometimes adding up to doses which are rather large for a child. Caffeine is the main ingredient in most look-alike pills.

Immediate Effects: Caffeine reduces fatigue, improves alertness and work output, mildly elevates moods, and suppresses the appetite. It constricts the blood vessels in the brain. This is the reason for its use in headache remedies. It increases urinary output, and stimulates the secretion of pepsin and hydrochloric acid in the stomach, causing gastric distress in some people.

Chronic Use: Chronic use of large amounts (600 mg. or more per day) can cause insomnia, restlessness, nervousness, anxiety, headaches, muscle twitching, diarrhea, increased urinary output, heart palpitations and stomach disorders. Some studies relate it to heart disease and also cystic breast disease in women. Convulsions and even death due to respiratory failure have been reported from very high doses, most often from look-alike pills.

REFERENCES FOR CAFFEINE: 41, 42.

INHALANTS

Inhalants are volatile substances inhaled intentionally for their intoxicating effects. They are often one of the first drugs of use. Inhalant use has been steadily increasing in both the younger and older teenage segments since 1980. In 1987, 18.6% of high school seniors reported they had gotten high on inhalants at least once in their lives. [44] Inhalant use is of grave concern because of its potential of permanent injury and death

Methods of Use: Inhalants may be sniffed (inhaled by nose) and/or huffed (inhaled by mouth). Users pour or spray the chemical into a plastic bag or balloon and then breathe in fumes through the nose and mouth, inhale the chemical that has been saturated on a rag or gauze, or they inhale the chemical directly from the original container or spray it directly into the mouth. The effect is immediate and the high is short so users often inhale repeatedly during each episode.

Death: Death may be caused by suffocation due to plastic bag inhalation techniques or "sudden sniffing death syndrome" (SSDS) resulting from cardiac complications. SSDS is more likely to occur when inhalation is done along with physical exertion or stress. The solvents and aerosol sprays are the chemicals most associated with SSDS.

Inhalants can be classed into three main categories: commercial solvents and aerosol sprays, anesthetics and the volatile nitrites.

Solvents and Aerosol Sprays

Some commonly abused items in this group are spray paints, hair sprays, vegetable oil sprays, cold weather car starters, air sanitizers, window cleaners, furniture polishes, insecticides, disinfectants, spray medications, deodorants, lighter fluid, butane, gasoline, transmission fluid, glues, paints, paint thinners, nail polish and removers, magic markers and shoe polish. Typewriter correction fluid and freon have emerged as current favorites of adolescents. These chemicals act as central nervous system depressants. Low doses may produce slight stimulation, moderate doses cause one to become uninhibited, and high doses can cause loss of consciousness and sometimes death. Other effects may be drowsiness, headaches, nausea, vision disturbances, watering of eyes, excess nasal secretions, coughing and salivation, chemical smell on the breath, sores on the nose and mouth, pallor, flushing and poor muscular control. Long term use can cause damage to the central nervous system, liver, kidneys, blood and bone marrow.

Anesthetics

Nitrous oxide (laughing gas), a general anesthetic, is legally sold as a propellant for whipped cream in an aerosol spray can or in small, unmarked, gray 8 gram metal cylinders called "Whippets." Whippets are sold with a balloon from which the gas is inhaled or a pipe ("Buzz Bomb") which combines with the cylinder. Adverse reactions from nitrous oxide can include shortness of breath, nausea, variations in heartbeat, and hearing loss. When inhaled directly from the cylinder, the lips and mouth can freeze. Long term use could cause nerve damage. Death is possible if the gas is inhaled without sufficient oxygen.

Volatile Nitrites

Amyl nitrite and butyl nitrite are used as a euphoriant and as a sexual stimulant. The high lasts only a few seconds to a minute, so users tend to inhale repeatedly during each sniffing episode. The nitrites temporarily dilate the blood vessels, causing the heart to beat harder and faster and fill the blood vessels with blood. Other effects include rapid pulse, headaches, dizziness, flushed face, lowered blood pressure, nausea and vomiting, fainting, and involuntary passing of urine and feces. Increased pressure in the eye with headaches can be a symptom of nitrite use rather than glaucoma. Long term use can cause an impetigo-like rash around the nose and mouth, hepatitis and brain hemorrhage. Amyl nitrite has a banana-like aroma. It is frequently sold in fragile glass ampules jacketed with cotton mesh material. The ampule is crushed in the hand and the chemical is absorbed into the fabric and inhaled. Hence, street names for amyl nitrite are "poppers" or "snappers." Some trade names for butyl nitrite, which is sold as a room odorizer, are Rush, Bolt, Locker Room, Bullet, Jac Aroma, Climax, Loc-A-Roma, Shotgun, Satan's Scent. The federal Anti-Drug Abuse Act of 1988, section 2404, bans Butyl Nitrite as a Banned Hazardous Substance.

REFERENCES FOR INHALANTS: 44, 45.

DEPRESSANTS

Substances classified as depressants under the Controlled Substance Act have a high potential for physical and psychological dependency with tolerance developing rapidly. On the street they are referred to as "downers" or "downs." Sedatives (sleeping pills) and tranquilizers are included in this classification. Most depressants are taken orally. These drugs are sometimes found in the home by teenagers who favor combining them with alcohol, a dangerous, sometimes fatal mistake.

Effects: Therapeutic low doses produce mild sedation and relief of anxiety, irritability and tension. Higher doses, used by abusers, may relieve anxiety, produce temporary euphoria or the other extreme of mood depression and apathy. They are often used to sooth "jangled nerves" brought on by stimulants, to soften "flashbacks," or to ease a withdrawal from heroin. Intoxicating doses can result in impaired judgement, slurred speech, distorted vision, and often unrealized loss of motor control, making driving dangerous. The user may be quarrelsome and appear intoxicated with no odor of alcohol. Large doses induce sleep and may cause stupor, respiratory depression, coma and even death.

Sedatives

Withdrawal: Withdrawal symptoms are more severe and dangerous than those of heroin addiction. Withdrawal should only be attempted in a controlled hospital environment.

Overdose: A moderate overdose resembles alcohol intoxication. A severe overdose causes dilated pupils, cold clammy skin, weak and rapid pulse, either slow or rapid breathing and possible coma.

Prescription Drugs Used as Street Drugs: Among the barbiturates are Nembutal, Seconal, Amytal, and Tuinal. Slang terms often indicate the color of the pills: barbs, bluebirds, blue devils, red birds, red devils, yellow jackets and yellows.

Non-barbiturate sedatives include Placidyl, Chloral Hydrate, Doriden, Noludar and Methaqualone (Quaalude). Methaqualone is no longer manufactured legally in the U.S.

Tranquilizers

Tranquilizers are the least toxic of the depressants but are highly addictive. Because they are fat soluble, they are eliminated from the body slowly. Withdrawal symptoms might not occur until 7 to 10 days after the drug is discontinued. They are used therapeutically to relieve muscle spasms and anxiety.

Some of the more common tranquilizers are Valium, Librium, Equanil, Miltown, Serax and Tranxene.

REFERENCES FOR DEPRESSANTS: 23, 33.

HALLUCINOGENS

Hallucinogens, are often called psychedelics or "consciousness expanding" drugs. "Bad trips" or panic reactions can occur even in experienced users. Hallucinogens are stored in fatty tissue including the brain. They are excreted very slowly. Tolerance develops rapidly. Withdrawal symptoms do not generally occur. Flashbacks, the recurrences of effects of the drug weeks, months, and even years after the last dose, are associated with hallucinogen use. The cause of flashbacks is unknown. Substances sold as hallucinogens are often PCP.

Effects: The effects may be different in each person with each administration, and can last for 6-14 hours. Hallucinogens affect perception, sensation, thinking and emotions. The user may have difficulty distinguishing between fact and fantasy and may hallucinate (see, hear or smell things that are not present). Other possible effects are dilated pupils, headaches, incoherent speech, lack of coordination, cold, sweaty hands and feet, vomiting, laughing, crying, shivering, goose pimples, irregular breathing, a strong body odor, and suicidal or homicidal tendencies. Acute anxiety, restlessness and sleeplessness are common until the drug wears off. Hallucinogens are stored in fatty tissue which is prevalent in the brain and are excreted very slowly. Chronic use can cause brain damage. Tolerance develops rapidly. There are no apparent physical withdrawal symptoms.

Persons in hallucinogenic states should be upset as little as possible to keep them from harming themselves or others.

LSD

Appearance and Methods of Use: Lysergic acid or LSD is once again a popular street drug, especially among adolescents. It is odorless, colorless, and tasteless. Doses of LSD are miniscule - an aspirin sized tablet makes 2 million hits. It is sold in the form of impregnated blotter paper ("blotter acid"), in brightly colored tablets (microdots), thin squares of gelatin ("window panes"), and less frequently as a clear liquid. The blotter acid (most popular form) is made up in sheets of stamps with designs or Disney type characters (especially attractive to children). It is put on the tongue or licked. The clear liquid drops and window panes can be put in the eye for quick absorption. They are damaging to the eye. Liquid drops are sometimes put on a sugar cube and taken orally. The hallucinogenic "trip" lasts for four to six hours.

Slang Terms: Acid, green or red dragon, paper acid, white lightning, blue heaven, purple haze, sugar cubes and blotter acid.

Mescaline

Mescaline is the active ingredient of the peyote cactus and is used as part of the religious rites of some American Indian tribes. It is sold as peyote buttons which are sliced off the plant and dried to form a hard brown disc. The buttons are chewed and swallowed and have a very foul taste. It is very irritating to the eyes requiring the protection of sunglasses for a week after usage. Synthetic mescaline is rarely found on the streets because of its very high cost.

Psilocybin and Psilocyn

Psilocybin and psilocyn are derived from certain mushrooms which are dried and brewed in a tea. The taste is very unpleasant. In some communities, mushrooms ("magic mushrooms" or "shrooms") are the hallucinogen of choice. Kits are available through drug culture magazines for growing mushrooms.

REFERENCES FOR HALLUCINOGENS: 1, 33.

PCP

Phencyclidine or PCP is related pharmacologically to hallucinogens and produces similar effects but some researchers consider it a separate class of drugs, because it produces different symptoms of tolerance and withdrawal. PCP is stored in fatty tissue which is prevalent in the brain. It is excreted very slowly. Flashbacks, the recurrences of effects of the drug weeks, months, and even years after the last dose, are associated with PCP use. The cause of flashbacks is unknown. Because it is so easily and inexpensively produced in bootleg laboratories it is often sold as another drug.

Appearance and Methods of Use: It is sold as a liquid, a white crystalline powder (angel dust), in capsules, or in pills called **PeaCe Pills** or "hogs," and smells like ether. PCP can be taken orally or injected but the preferred route is smoking it after being sprayed on cigarettes, parsley or marijuana. The liquid is sometimes dropped in the eye for faster absorption which can damage the eye. One ounce of PCP yields 30-40 dime ($10) bags or foil packets.

Slang Terms: Killer weed, green, tac, ozone, DOA (dead on arrival), embalming fluid, rocket fuel, supergrass and elephant tranquilizer. PCP sprayed on marijuana is called lovely, boat, or loveboat. A sherm is a cigarette sprayed with PCP.

Effects: The effects of PCP can vary greatly and can last from 3-14 hours. It can cause a sense of detachment, distance, and estrangement from the user's surroundings, numbness, slurred or blocked speech, and a loss of coordination accompanied by a sense of strength and invulnerability. The user may have a blank stare, rapid and involuntary eye movements, and an exaggerated gait. Auditory hallucinations, image distortion, and severe mood disorders may occur, producing acute anxiety, a feeling of impending doom, or paranoia and violent hostility. High doses can cause muscle rigidity, rapid and irregular heart beat, convulsions and coma.

Diagnosis of PCP use is frequently missed because the user often looks normal. But, even though he may look normal, the user still may become very violent and exhibit bizarre behavior, injuring himself or those around him. There are several reasons for this. Physical strength can be greatly increased under the influence of PCP. Police report instances of users breaking handcuffs and becoming very violent. The drug is an anesthetic and numbs the user so he does not feel physical harm he may do to himself. The drug is also an amnesic so the user may not remember what he did under the influence of the drug. More deaths are caused by the resultant behavior than from the physical effects of the drug. Psychotic behavior may continue for as long as two weeks after a single dose.

PCP is one of the most dangerous of all drugs. Persons under the influence of PCP should be upset as little as possible to keep them from harming themselves or others.

Long Term Effects: Long term use can affect memory, judgment, concentration and perception. Chronic users can become psychotic, paranoic, and exhibit schizophrenic behavior. Chronic PCP use is often misdiagnosed as paranoid-schizophrenia.

REFERENCES FOR PCP: 1, 2, 33.

NARCOTICS

The term narcotics refers to opium, its derivatives, and synthetic substitutes. Narcotics are physically and psychologically addictive drugs. Tolerance develops rapidly. In professional medicine, they are the most effective pain relievers known. The intravenous route, "mainlining," is preferred by abusers.

Effects: Besides euphoria, other effects may include drowsiness, stupor, poor co-ordination, confusion, watery eyes, pinpoint pupils, loss of appetite, slowed breathing and pulse rate, nausea, constipation and excessive itching.

Chronic Addiction: Chronic use can lead to psychosocial deterioration, malnutrition, neglect of general health, infections from contaminated syringes at sites of injections, blood infection, hepatitis, AIDS or endocarditis.

Withdrawal: Physical withdrawal symptoms begin two to four hours after the last dose of the drug and peak 36 to 72 hours later. They subside in seven to ten days. Symptoms include watery eyes, runny nose, yawning, perspiration, restlessness, irritability, loss of appetite, insomnia, goose flesh, tremors, severe sneezing, nausea, vomiting, stomach cramps and diarrhea. The heart rate and blood pressure are elevated, and chills alternate with flushing and excessive sweating. Pains in the bones and muscle spasms with kicking movements probably led to the expression, "kicking the habit." The user is weak and depressed and may be suicidal.

Overdose: Symptoms are deep sleep, stupor, slow shallow breathing, cold clammy skin, limp body, and a relaxed jaw. Coma and/or convulsions can occur. Death may result from respiratory depression.

Heroin: It is the narcotic favored by abusers because it gives the most intense "high." Heroin is a powder which may range in color from white to dark brown. A new more potent, cheaper form, "black tar," is sticky like tar or hard like coal. Intravenous (injected into a vein) use is preferred but it may also be sniffed, smoked (chasing the dragon), or injected under the skin, (skin popping). The high purity of today's heroin is popularizing the sniffing method.

Slang Terms: Big H, boy, brown sugar, snow, stuff, junk, smack, scag and horse. P dope, Passion, Power, Body Bag, Liberty and Blue Thunder are trade names. Speedball is heroin combined with cocaine.

Methadone: Methadone is a synthetic narcotic which is used to treat heroin addicts who are unable to stay drug free. It is used in place of heroin because it produces a much less intense high allowing many addicts to lead a productive life while maintained on methadone. Methadone is sometimes abused.

Other Frequently Abused Narcotics: Morphine, Demerol, Dilaudid, and Percodan may be taken orally but injection is preferred. Opium may be smoked through a long stemmed pipe. Opium is also present in antidiarrhea over-the-counter preparations such as paregoric.

Codeine is less addictive and produces less euphoria than the above drugs. It is usually taken orally in preparations combined with Empirin Compound, Aspirin, or Tylenol. Codeine also acts as a cough suppressant and is found in some cough medicines such as Robitussin AC, Cheracol, and Elixir of Terpin Hydrate with Codeine. While Codeine is generally not preferred by narcotic addicts, it should be noted that it is a drug often present in many homes of adolescents who are using drugs. It should be kept in a locked container.

Darvon and Talwin are pain relievers, not classed as narcotics, but their misuse has caused them to be regulated by the Controlled Substance Act.

REFERENCES FOR NARCOTICS: 33, 41.

DESIGNER DRUGS

A new drug abuse problem is the so-called "designer drugs." These drugs are synthetic compounds made by underground chemists by altering the molecular structure of mind-altering drugs. Since the drug laws define illegal drugs by their exact molecular structure, the newly altered molecule is legal (i.e. not illegal). When the Drug Enforcement Administration (DEA) outlaws a designer drug, chemists go on to make another new analog or derivative.

Changing the molecular structure of a drug can change its potency, length of action, euphoric effects, and toxicity. Produced in clandestine laboratories, designer drugs are likely to contain contaminants. Overdoses are common and numerous deaths have been attributed to them. The most common groups of designer drugs are described below.

Analogs Of Amphetamine

MDMA, (ecstacy) and its parent, MDA, are analogs of amphetamine. Ecstasy produces intoxication along with increased acoustic, visual, and tactile (touch) perceptions. There are a number of negative side effects which include psychotic episodes, nausea, vomiting and fluctuations in blood pressure and heart rate. Researchers have found brain damage from as little as one dose. Other names for ecstasy are X, XTC, essence, and adam.

Analogs Of Fentanyl

Fentanyl is an analgesic used in anesthesia. Hundreds of analogs are possible, some with properties very similar to heroin. At least five analogs have been on the streets and identified by the Drug Enforcement Administration (DEA). They are sold as Asian heroin or marketed under various street names including China White, Mexican Heroin, synthetic dope and gasoline dope. It looks exactly like heroin, requires very miniscule doses for an intense high, and is 20 to 40 times stronger than heroin. Many overdose deaths have been attributed to it.

Analogs Of Meperidine

Some analogs of meperidine (Demerol) are MPTP, MPPP, and PEPAP. They produce effects similar to heroin. The most well known one is MPTP (new heroin) which also causes Parkinson disease-like symptoms such as stiffness, impaired speech, rigidity, tremors, and sometimes paralysis. It causes irreversible brain damage.

Analogs Of PCP

Over 35 analogues of PCP have been synthesized. Some are already regulated as a controlled substance.

REFERENCES FOR DESIGNER DRUGS: 34, 40, 46.

OVER-THE-COUNTER DRUGS

Over-the-counter (OTC) drugs are preparations which can be purchased without a prescription. Some of them have mind-altering capabilities. While they are relatively harmless if used as directed, in large amounts they can produce a high and other harmful side effects. Many have a potential for harm if used unscrupulously over an extended period of time or in combination with other medications or street drugs. They are easily purchased or shoplifted. Cough medicines with synthetic codeine are heavily abused in some communities. OTC drugs and prescription drugs found in the home medicine cabinet are often ingested, shared, or sold by adolescents. Those with mind-altering properties may contain antihistamines and/or sympathomimetic agents.

Antihistamines

Antihistamines are found in cold remedies, cough syrups, sleep aids, allergy preparations, anti-itching agents, motion sickness relievers, and analgesics. Side effects include drowsiness, dizziness, dryness of the mouth, and disturbed coordination. However, some users will experience excitement symptoms such as insomnia, nervousness and even convulsions.

Sympathomimetic Agents

Some of the drugs in this classification are ephedrine, amphetamines, phenylephrine, naphazoline and phenylpropanolamine. They are used in anti-asthmatic preparations for bronchial dilation; nasal sprays and cough or cold remedies; weight reducing agents; and in synthetic cocaine preparations. Effects include stimulation of the central nervous system, constriction of the arterioles (which causes shrinkage of the mucous membranes to relieve nasal congestion), increased blood pressure and heart rate, dilation of the pupils, dilation of the bronchials, nausea, headache, and anxiety.

Clove Cigarettes

"Kreteks," or clove cigarettes, produce a mild high and have been a rapidly growing fad in the United States since about 1980. Kreteks contain 60% tobacco and 40% cloves. Cloves contain a natural anesthetic called eugenol which has been used for many years for temporary relief of toothaches. Cloves or oil of clove preparations seem to have no ill effects when used orally. The burning of eugenol however, seems to either have a direct toxic effect on the respiratory system by immobilizing the infection-fighting cells allowing viruses and bacteria to run rampant, or by causing an acute allergic reaction. Users have complained of coughing up blood, nosebleeds, shortness of breath, nausea, infections and asthma.

REFERENCES FOR OVER-THE-COUNTER DRUGS: 41, 47, 48.

LOOK-ALIKES

Look-alikes are low potency preparations made to look like controlled substances, mainly stimulants (uppers) and depressants (downers). New laws banning look-alikes have prompted manufacturers to make pills that no longer look like controlled substances. They are sold in bottles of 100 or 1,000 in stores and through mail order houses, providing a young seller a very high profit margin. The "legal stimulants" usually contain caffeine alone or in combination with ephedrine. The amount of caffeine in look-alikes varies from 37 mg. to 324 mg. One cup of coffee contains 85-100 mg. of caffeine. The "legal downers" usually contain antihistamines.

Although look-alikes may seem innocuous, their use entices a child to try drugs. To get a high, kids quickly learn they must ingest several of these pills, or even a handful. There is a danger that a child accustomed to the weak "copy-cat" drug will unknowingly buy the authentic drug, take several pills, and overdose. Each of the ingredients in look-alikes is dangerous when taken in sufficient quantities. Deaths have been associated with these drugs.

ANABOLIC STEROIDS

Anabolic steroids, the so-called body building drugs, are synthetic testosterone-like drugs which have anabolic (tissue building) properties, and androgenic (masculinizing) properties. Anabolic steroids are always androgenic. They are also mind-altering drugs. They are taken orally or injected intramuscularly.

Vast quantities of illicit anabolic steroids are imported from Mexico and Europe. The Mexican drugs are predominantly counterfeits of unknown composition. Imported anabolic steroids are subject to seizure by the U.S. Customs Service. Sold under the names of Anovar, Deca-Durabolin, Dianabol, Durabolin, Pimobolin, and others, the misuse of these drugs has grown to such proportions among some athletes that in certain sports experts feel that it is now unlikely that non-users can actually compete in these particular arenas on a world class level. Athletes are sometimes given anabolic steroids in the guise of vitamins or food supplements.

The American College of Medicine warns that there is no conclusive evidence that extremely large doses of anabolic-androgenic steroids either aid or hinder athletic performance, and that they are potentially dangerous taken in large doses (a tendency among athletes) over an extended period of time.

Effects: In adolescents, anabolic steroids cause a closing of the growth plate at the ends of the long bones, thereby permanently stunting growth. Anabolic steroids change the body's electrolyte balance causing retention of sodium, which in turn causes the body to retain fluids, so that much of the desired weight gain is caused not by muscle build up, but by retained fluids. Physicians who prescribe anabolic steroids for athletic injuries may actually be prolonging the damage, since in many cases the chemicals delay the normal healing process, due to their suppressive effect on the immune system. The use of these drugs can even *contribute to* injuries, because athletes who use them are too big and aggressive for their natural body size, and consequently, they may injure other athletes. Anabolic steroids tend to make muscles grow, but not the connective tendons and ligaments, which results in extra stress on the tendons and ligaments.

Anabolic steroids can cause jaundice (yellowing of the skin), liver damage, high blood pressure, and endocrine imbalance. Some studies associate cancer of the liver with anabolic steroid use. In males they can cause enlarged breasts, a decrease in testicular size and function, and a decrease of sperm production. Females can experience acne, menstrual irregularities and irreversible masculinizing effects such as hair on the face, deepening of the voice, or a change in the genitals.

Psychological effects can include mood elevation or depression, increase or decrease in sex drive, increased aggressive behavior, and occasional psychotic episodes.

Withdrawal: During withdrawal a user may experience depression, manic-like symptoms, insomnia, loss of energy or appetite, nausea, and headaches for one to three weeks. A weight loss of 10-25% of body weight will occur.

REFERENCES FOR ANABOLIC STEROIDS: 49.

EFFECTS OF DRUGS ON THE FETUS

The addiction and birth defects occurring from prenatal exposure to drugs is a new form of child abuse. Alcohol and most drugs go through the placental barrier to the baby and can affect the developing fetus during all stages of pregnancy. The dose received by the fetus is an adult dose or close to it, taxing the immature organs which metabolize and excrete the offending substance. Evidence of heroin, morphine, cocaine, and marijuana can be found in infant stools up to five days after birth. After birth, alcohol and most drugs used by the mother pass into the mother's milk.

Miscarriage, prematurity, complications of labor, still birth, and low birth weight occur more frequently in mothers who have used alcohol or other drugs during pregnancy. Drugs used by mothers have a direct toxic effect on development of the fetal immune system. The thalamus and right temporal lobe in the brain tend to be smaller in newborns of drug-using mothers. There is evidence that alcohol and other drugs can damage the ovum or sperm of users. Researchers are just beginning to determine long term behavioral and developmental effects of prenatal exposure to drugs.

Babies exposed to drugs prenatally are often born addicted and experience a withdrawal syndrome called Neonatal Abstinence Syndrome (NAS). They exhibit increased sensitivity to noise, irritability, poor coordination, excessive sneezing and yawning, and uncoordinated sucking and swallowing reflexes. Symptoms may persist for two to three weeks.

Alcohol: Research indicates that even small amounts of alcohol can harm the fetus. Fetal Alcohol Syndrome (FAS) is a set of birth defects that can result from heavy drinking during pregnancy. One, several, or all of the following defects may occur: central nervous system abnormalities such as mental retardation, abnormal brain development, poor motor coordination, poor muscle tone, or hyperactivity; distinctive facial features like short eyelid fissures, short upturned nose, no groove between the nose and upper lip, a thin upturned upper lip, and retarded growth of the jaws; growth deficiencies in both length and weight before and after birth; malformations of the heart, genitals, urinary system and the skeleton. FAS is the third leading cause of mental retardation present at birth.

Marijuana: The FAS facial features have also been reported in babies whose mothers used marijuana. Babies of marijuana using mothers are more likely to have one or more major malformation than babies of non-users. [31]

Cocaine: Babies of cocaine users have a higher than normal incidence of kidney, respiratory, and visual problems, lack of co-ordination, and developmental problems. They are prone to temper tantrums, hyperactivity and developmental problems described in the PCP babies.

Nicotine: Tobacco use is associated with increased incidence of miscarriage, prematurity, and low birth weights. Nicotine causes constriction of the blood vessels which carry oxygen and nutrients to the developing baby. Carbon monoxide replaces the oxygen in the blood, further jeopardizing the baby. This oxygen deficiency is considered a cause of the behavioral abnormalities such as hyperactivity, short attention span, and lower spelling and reading tests, which occurred more in children of smokers than non-smokers. [39]

PCP: During the first six weeks, babies of PCP users tend to have more medical problems, especially respiratory distress. They display sudden outbursts of agitation, tremors, darting eye movements, and rapid changes in the level of consciousness, similar to a user's reaction to PCP. A study done during an 18-month period on the growth of infants exposed prenatally to PCP showed demonstrated borderline abilities in fine motor, adaptive, language and personal-social development. [43]

Opiates: Babies born to opiate users exhibit many of the same characteristics as the PCP babies.

REFERENCES FOR EFFECTS ON THE FETUS:
5, 19, 21, 24, 31, 32, 38, 39, 43

4 PREVENTION IN THE FAMILY

Kids try alcohol and other drugs for the same reasons their parents and grandparents tried cigarettes and alcohol. In contrast to the past, use today is more extensive and begins earlier. Chemicals are now marketed more intensely, are easier to obtain and are available in more varieties. Research described below indicates that (1) attitudes about alcohol and other drug use are already being formed by children during their grade school years; (2) many children are offered alcohol and other drugs during their preteen years; (3) the media, siblings and friends are major influences towards usage; and (4) the younger that use starts, the more serious the problem becomes. To be most effective, prevention education and attitude formation must begin at a very young age. The primary prevention responsibility lies within the family by those persons who care for, protect, and nurture the child. The efforts of schools, communities and the government are greatly diminished without the support of strong, healthy families.

SURVEY FINDINGS

Many surveys have been taken concerning drug use and attitudes about drug use which furnish useful information and help to indicate trends and patterns of use. Two surveys are discussed below that identify some of the causes of alcohol and other drug use and give some clues for planning prevention in our homes and communities.

The 1987 *Weekly Reader* National Survey on Drugs and Drinking

The *Weekly Reader* questioned children's attitudes and perceptions (not actual usage) about alcohol and other drug use. Children were surveyed in grades four through twelve from urban, suburban, and rural schools across the country. The figures below focus on fourth through sixth graders.

What Makes Drug Use Attractive? TV and movies was the greatest influence on fourth through sixth graders for making alcohol and other drugs seem like fun. Peer pressure was the second strongest influence.

Why Do Kids Use Alcohol and Other Drugs? In the survey, choices of main reasons were to (1) feel older, (2) have a good time, (3) get over feeling bad (self-medication), (4) fit in with other kids (peer pressure), and

(5) some other reason. "Fitting in with others" was the leading reason for using alcohol and marijuana for grades four to six, and "having a good time" for high school students. "To feel older" was the second main reason for grades four through six.

Peer Pressure: Forty-one percent of fourth graders reported peer pressure to try cigarettes, 34% to try wine coolers, 36% other alcohol, 25% to try marijuana and 24% to try cocaine or crack. Among sixth graders, 58% said kids their age push each other to try cigarettes, 46% to try wine coolers, 51% other alcohol, 34% marijuana, and 31% cocaine.

Substances Perceived as a Drug: Cigarettes were perceived as a drug by 37% of fourth to sixth graders, compared to 24% in 1983. While 45% of fourth to sixth graders considered beer, wine, or liquor as a drug, only 21% believed the same of wine coolers. The perception of alcohol as a drug increased 11% from 1983. Marijuana was perceived as a drug by 91%. The perception of the ***harmfulness*** of alcohol dropped after fourth grade and for marijuana it fell after the sixth grade.

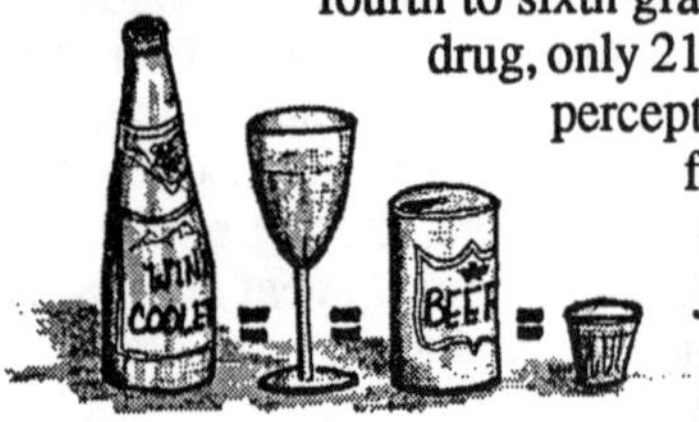

Chuck *. . . "I started getting high off pot when I was 11 with my best friend. He was two years older and I really wanted to be like him. My friend's 16-year-old brother did drugs and we would steal his drugs and get high. I did it at first to keep from being called chicken or being left out. For almost two years my parents were not fully aware I used drugs. I was sneaky and a good "con," which kept me from getting caught."*

Jim *. . . "I began experimenting with marijuana at the end of eighth grade. Basically, I wanted to try the drug because my friends had said the sensation of being "high" was very pleasurable. I believed, along with my friends, that smoking pot regularly was relatively harmless; and it certainly was no worse than cigarettes or alcohol. By the time I was smoking pot regularly, I must say I was having a fun time. I was part of a group that would go to parties and get high and/or drunk. As stupid as it may seem, this was my way of truly having a good time. Marijuana, through my experiences, provided me with a lot of pleasure. Being an avid fan of rock music, getting high and listening to this music was a great lift. Going to rock concerts had the same affect. Marijuana was a great way to make friends. I wasn't considered "cool" or "with it" unless I got "stoned." Pot was a way of communicating with others. If I got a friend high I could relate to that person better. I didn't feel inhibited, and I could open up to that person much easier than if I was straight."*

The Partnership for a Drug-Free America 1987 and 1988 Surveys

The Partnership for a Drug-Free America has targeted marijuana, cocaine and crack in its anti-drug advertising campaign. The Partnership conducted nationwide surveys both in 1987 and in 1988 in order to provide information that would assist in the design of the ads and measure their effectiveness. All ages from 9 years old and up were surveyed. Respondents were recruited at shopping malls and other central locations from coast to coast. College students were surveyed on 130 college campuses.

Older Sibling Influence: The influence of older siblings is the single strongest predictor of early vulnerability to drug use of 9-to-12-year-olds. This is not a role that the older drug-using sibling wishes to play. 60% of marijuana using teenagers and 66% of cocaine using teens greatly fear influencing their younger siblings with their drug use.

Peer Group Influences: Peer group associations are the second most influential predictors of usage for preteens and teenagers. This relationship is so strong that teenagers who associate with friends who use drugs probably use drugs themselves. Among the 9-to-12-year-olds, 39% say it's hard to say no to a friend, 37% believe drug users are popular, 31% think drug users have many friends, and 13% have friends who already use marijuana. Among teenagers, 29% see drug users as popular, 28% believe drugs are just a part of growing up, 22% agree its fun to have drugs at parties, and 11% feel it's all right to sell cocaine to a friend.

Availability: In the 9-to-12-year-old group, 16% were approached to buy or use drugs in 1987 and 18% were approached in 1988. 15% agree it is easy to get marijuana, and 7% say cocaine is easy to get. Ease of obtaining drugs increases with age. Among 13-year-olds, 13% report it's easy or fairly easy to obtain cocaine. The percentage increases to 38% for 16- and 17-year-olds.

Scott . . . *"I used to grow pot in the woods near my friend's house, but never enough to sell. I sold drugs to make money but mainly so I could use the profits to get high myself. I would sell speed, hash, cocaine and pot, mostly at school and around the neighborhood hangouts. When I needed drugs I would buy them mainly at school, but I also could go to the hangouts and wait till a dealer would show up. When I first started using drugs on a regular basis I would spend $15 a week on drugs, but when I got older and had a job I would spend $50 or more a week on drugs and at times $150."*

Bob . . . *"I used to buy and sell drugs almost anywhere that there were people my age, like school, work, shopping centers and parties. I also stole* *drugs and stole checks, gold and silver from home. During my worst usage I probably spent from $75 to $200 a week on drugs. I got arrested as a juvenile for forging checks."*

Age of First Use: The age of first use and age of first regular use strongly predicts the future use of marijuana and cocaine. The younger drug use begins, the more severe the drug problem will become. By age 13, 12% of teenagers have tried marijuana, and 8% have tried cocaine.

Deterrents to Drug Use: All age groups feared getting caught by the law or by their loved ones more than the harmful effects of drugs. One exception is the adult cocaine user who fears dying from crack use more than getting caught. Regular church attendance is strongly related to much lower levels of drug use among all populations.

Teenage and Adult Drug Use: The 18-to-35-age group has the highest rate of drug use. Use peaks at about age 28. Marijuana was used during the past year by 29.7% of 13-to-17-year-old teenagers, 43.4% of high school seniors, 32.3% of college students, and 42.5% of young adults aged 18 to 27 years old. Cocaine was used during the past year by 11.1% of 13-to-17-year-old teenagers, 15.2% of high school seniors, 14% of college students, and 19.9% of young adults aged 18 to 27 years old. Women today are nearly identical to men in their use of marijuana and cocaine.

Adult Attitudes: Among college students who support continued drug use, 32% see drug users as no different from others; 27% believe that using cocaine is a status symbol; 22% feel that drugs help you forget your troubles; and 21% say parties are more fun with drugs.

Among other adults who support drug use, 29% think cigarettes are worse than pot; 26% think its OK to smoke pot in private; 20% feel that cocaine is a status symbol; and 11% feel that occasional cocaine use is not risky.

Parental Attitudes: Attitudes of parents make it more difficult for them to prevent and identify drug use among their children. Among the parents surveyed, 51% think their kids will never take drugs; 43% think their kids don't have the money to buy drugs; 31% think their kids have never been exposed to drugs; only 34% believe their kids will actually try drugs; 50% believe their kids have never tried drugs; but 61% report that drugs have affected children they know.

Effectiveness of the Media Campaign: The 1988 survey attempted to assess attitudinal changes since the Partnership's anti-drug advertising campaign began in 1987. Ten selected media areas around the U.S. received four times more advertising than other areas. Many attitudes became distinctly more antagonistic toward drug use in all of the samples. Positive changes were most pronounced in the college sample, followed by children aged 9 to 12. Of all the age groups, teenagers experienced the least attitudinal shifts. There was no significant increase in views sympathetic to drug use. Among college students, there was a significant decline in cocaine use by the occasional users. There was no decline in marijuana or cocaine use in any other age groups.

In the areas with high media exposure the attitudinal changes were substantially greater on most variables than in the balance of the country. The survey data strongly suggests that advertising affects attitudes about drug use but it has to reach a threshold before it begins to have much effect.

PREVENTION WITHIN THE FAMILY

Today, outside influences often outweigh the positive influences of parents, churches and teachers. Parents have to work harder than ever to build a healthy family structure that will give children the tools to make good decisions. Even in a strong family unit a child may make inappropriate choices, but early intervention and successful recovery will be more likely.

The tools of prevention are essentially the same as the tools of recovery: (1) working on self, (2) strengthening the marriage and the family relationships, (3) development of good coping techniques and communication and social skills, (4) alternative recreational activities, (5) drug education of parents and children and (6) avoidance of potentially harmful situations.

Family Vulnerability to Chemical Dependency: Research now indicates that some alcoholism has a genetic component. Family environmental factors also strongly influence the occurrence of chemical dependency. Anyone who has been raised in a family with a chemically dependent person is at risk of becoming chemically dependent, marrying an alcoholic, or being the parent of a chemically dependent child. Chapter 2 describes behaviors which are learned in childhood that make family members more vulnerable to ongoing problems. Attendance at Al-Anon meetings, Adult Children of Alcoholics meetings, or therapy with a chemical dependency counselor can help such persons correct those behaviors that promote chemical dependency. (See Resource Section). Children should be made aware of their family backgrounds and possible genetic tendencies.

A Good Example Is the Best Sermon: The parents' total life style, attitudes, and methods of dealing with problems are influential examples that children will use in their own approach to life. A personal inventory of strengths and weaknesses can give parents insight into improving their own physical, mental and spiritual life. Journaling one's thoughts and progress is very helpful. Some personal questions to ask relating to positive role model character traits include:

Am I satisfied with my direction in life?

Do I keep all aspects of my life in good balance?

Do I have realistic goals and accept the fact that life is not perfect?

Do I spend time on my spiritual life?

Am I the kind of person I want my child to be?

Do I show care towards others?

Can I love unconditionally?

Am I judgmental?

Can I accept others as they are?

Do I display positive attitudes?

Am I honest? Dishonesty includes the information left out and the secrets kept to protect self or others. Secrets sustain and nurture problems.

Do I have good problem solving skills?

Am I manipulative - blame others for problems, lay guilt trips on others, do sneaky things, or throw tantrums to get my way?

Do I take responsibility for my actions?

Do I admit it when I've made a mistake?

Am I a good listener?

Do I try to control and dictate to others?

Am I patient with others?

Do I need material things for happiness?

Do I seek instant gratification?

Am I able to tolerate small amounts of discomfort without medication?

Do I self-medicate with alcohol, prescription or street drugs? Self-medication is indicated by the need for a drink to relax after work, to have a good time at a party, or to face an unpleasant situation.

A Healthy Marital Relationship Helps: The parents' marriage relationship is another type of role model that children observe and on which, they base their relationships. Children get messages regarding supportiveness, care, allowance for individualism, unity, honesty, handling of disagreements, enjoyment of each other, and expression of feelings within the marriage. Sooner or later, parents will have disagreements about solutions to teenage problems. If they cannot communicate well, reach an agreement, and present a united front to the children, chaos results. There is no feeling of security for the child, and the child is invited to satisfy his/her wants by manipulation of the parents. This controlling behavior is then extended to other relationships.

Single Parents Have Special Needs: In families where parents are separated or divorced, children need to know that the breakup was not the children's fault. Special precautions are necessary to guard against blame, guilt and anger towards the other parent. If both parents are still involved in the child's life, a united front is extremely important. A child who has lost a parent through death needs to be able to verbalize feelings about it. The child may have an irrational fear of the second parent dying. Children tend to blame themselves for anything negative that happens in their family, including a death. A subtle "no-talk" rule in the family can sustain this unjustified, crippling guilt and inhibit the child from ever learning to share feelings in a healthy way. Single parents are in special need of outside support systems and other adult companionship. Since empty homes are prime locations for adolescent chemical use, special attention is needed for monitoring children's whereabouts while working parents are absent from home.

Strong Families Have Teamwork: In a healthy family there is a team spirit and each member feels comfortable talking about feelings, problems and moral issues with family members. They receive positive feedback, feel unconditional love despite character defects or past actions, and take responsibility for their actions. Good listening skills help avoid poor, impulsive, and unfair or insensitive decisions. Parents should carefully examine situations to determine if they are required to make a decision or just need to provide parental guidance to help the child improve decision-making skills. Good behavior receives more recognition than bad behavior. A message of care and love accompanies consequences for unacceptable behavior. Members support each other, make sacrifices for each other, realize their role modeling responsibilities, and spend quality time together. Children are encouraged to bring friends home. A good family relationship does not happen in a day, week or month, it is an ongoing deliberate process. Honesty, acceptance, forgiveness and humility are all part of the process.

Rights and Responsibilities: In a family, the rights and responsibilities of parents and children need to be clearly defined. Each right has corresponding responsibilities. It is more important for parents to be a parent than a best friend to their child. Parents' responsibilities include establishing family values, nurturing, providing structure, supervision and health care. Household responsibilities and chores foster self discipline and build self esteem and feelings of self worth. Tough love, a consistently enforced set of household rules and consequences for undesirable behavior are essential to the child's development from the earliest age. Behavior rules and limits should be imposed before things have gone wrong. Curfews, monitoring of TV and movies, and rules for telephone and car use and party attendance are not unreasonable. Freedoms and privileges, such as driving and dating, need not be bestowed until they are earned and a child has shown enough maturity to handle them responsibly. Money is less likely to be spent on drugs if the child must earn spending money and be financially responsible for some necessities of life.

Awareness of Enabling Behaviors: Many of the enabling behaviors discussed in Chapter 2 begin during the early parenting years. They are done with much care and good intentions, but in reality they actually tear down what the parent is trying so hard to build. Children need to be allowed to fail and experience the consequences of their actions at a young age. Parents should not rescue their kids by lying for them, or bailing them out of trouble at school or in the neighborhood. Parental support of discipline imposed by school authorities and other forms of authority is important. The *LETTING GO* poem on page 38 is a good set of guidelines. [11]

Tell It Like It Is: When parents can express their own frustrations, verbalize their shortcomings, and talk through a problem solution with their children, the children learn that it's all right to have problems, that no one is perfect, and that chemicals are not necessary to handle difficulties.

Leisure Time: Children need to learn enjoyable alternatives to alcohol and drug use such as sports, music, theater, hobbies, reading, or appreciation of nature, by observing their parents' use of leisure time and sharing some of the activities with them.

A "No Use" Stand Is a Clear Message: The surest form of prevention is never to begin experimentation. If parents give the message that they expect their children to experiment with alcohol and drugs, they are more apt to do so. For those under the legal drinking age, there is no such thing as "responsible use" of alcohol. Responsible use of alcohol by adults is drinking in moderation without getting high and no drivng after any drinking. There is no such thing as "responsible or recreational use" of other drugs for anyone. Many kids who have stayed straight attribute it, at least in part, to their parents' "no use" stand and strong consequences for use. Parents must reject the negative peer pressure of other parents and take a stand of their own. Involvement in anti-drug community activities portrays a strong no use message.

Alcohol and Other Drug Education: Alcohol and other drug education for parents is just as important as the children's education. One of the most important segments of parent education is the realization of children's vulnerability and exposure to drugs. The younger a child begins alcohol and other drug use the more severe the problem will become. Kids are less likely to try alcohol and other drugs if they know their parents are informed, cannot be easily deceived and have taken a no use stand. When parents know the signs and symptoms of use, early recognition and intervention is more likely before the problem becomes serious. Professionals now advise parents not "to teach kids how to drink." There is evidence that alcohol can be harmful to the developing body and a possible genetic predisposition to alcoholism is not detectable.

The 1988 National High School Survey indicates that drug education is effective. Even though the availability of marijuana has remained stable since 1975, adolescent marijuana use has been slowly decreasing in direct proportion to the kids' perception of the harmfulness of regular marijuana use. But still more education is imperative as evidenced by the **Partnership's** finding that 25% of teenagers believe pot increases creativity and 24% don't know or don't believe that cocaine is risky.

It seems to be more difficult to achieve a change in beliefs and use patterns of two other gateway drugs, tobacco and alcohol. The **PRIDE 1987-88 National Summary** shows that 88% of teenagers perceive cigarettes as being harmful to health. Yet, the **High School Survey** reported that there has been no significant decline in teenage tobacco use since 1980, and 28.7% of high school seniors smoked cigarettes during the past 30 days. Smokeless tobacco use has increased substantially among young men. Teenage alcohol use has not declined since 1975. The **PRIDE** data found alcohol is perceived by sixth through twelfth graders as less harmful to health than cigarettes and other drugs.

Any alcohol or drug literature intended for children should be checked for accuracy and for "soft on drugs" or "responsible use attitudes." There is a surprising amount of unsuitable materials in our schools and libraries. Literature funded by the tobacco or alcohol industry should be very carefully scrutinized. Sources of appropriate reading materials and books are listed in the Resource Section.

Tobacco Use a Strong Predictor of Other Drug Use: In his book, **Getting Tough on Gateway Drugs,** Dr. Robert DuPont states, *"Twelve-to-17-year-olds who are current smokers of cigarettes, when compared to youths of the same age who do not smoke, are twice as likely to be current users of alcohol, nine times as likely to make illegal use of pills such as stimulants and tranquilizers, 10 times as likely to smoke marijuana, and 14 times as likely to use cocaine, heroin or hallucinogens. Thus, current smoking of cigarettes is a strong predictor of other drug use among teenagers. One conclusion: prevention of cigarette smoking is a high priority in the prevention of dependence on all drugs."* [2, pg. 32] This role of tobacco use (smoked or smokeless) is in all age groups, but is especially pronounced when use is initiated at age seventeen or younger. Alcohol use is a strong predictor of other drug use, but tobacco is an even stronger predictor of other drug use. [39] The **PRIDE** data indicates that 75% of teenage tobacco users started tobacco use under the age of fourteen. [6]

The Drugs of Early Use: Tobacco, inhalants, alcohol and marijuana are the first drugs kids use. Since 1980, inhalant use has been increasing in both the younger and older teenage segments. It is of grave concern because of its potential of permanent injury and death.

Alcohol tends to be used earlier than marijuana. The **PRIDE** data shows beer was used by 34% and liquor by 19.2% of sixth to eighth graders. In that study the current junior high students used beer at a younger age than the current high school students. The drugs of choice for most adolescents who use are alcohol and marijuana. As drug use progresses, cocaine, other stimulants and hallucinogens may be added to the menu. In most communities heroin is not part of the adolescent scene.

Know the Current Teenage Scene: To gain awareness of the adolescent world, listen to the lyrics of heavy metal rock music and to the kids' favorite "DJ's," watch the music videos that are popular with the kids, and study record album jackets. Parents should be able to identify drug paraphernalia. Frequently used terms are "doing drugs," "partying," or "to party." They all mean to drink and take drugs.

The **PRIDE** data reports that the most frequent places kids drink alcohol and do drugs are in their own homes or a friend's home. If there is a home alcohol supply it should not be accessible to adolescents. Cars are another favorite place to drink and drug. Teenagers can easily buy alcohol with or without fake ID's. Kids purchase beer from young adults who "pimp for beer" on parking lots of convenience stores. Wine coolers are marketed to appear as though they have little or no alcohol content and are displayed in some stores next to the soft drinks. The fact is, a bottle of wine cooler has the same alcohol content as a can of beer.

Keg parties are held at homes where the parents may or may not be present. Many parents buy kegs of beer for teen parties with the excuse that "at least they aren't doing drugs," or "at least they aren't out on the street." Drugs are usually available at these parties. Keg parties are often advertised by passing out flyers at high schools and sometimes at intermediate schools. It is advisable for parents to check out parties before they allow their teens to attend them. Parental guidelines and a parent pledge program for alcohol- and drug-free parties are described in Chapter 5 and the Resource Section.

Drug dealers live within walking distance of most schools. Drugs are sold by students on school grounds. Smoking courts, bathrooms, and secluded corners are preferred selling areas. The arcades, hallways and restrooms of shopping centers are prime places for selling drugs. Many record stores and street vendors sell drug paraphernalia. Some home medicine cabinets offer a supply of mind-altering prescription drugs.

Kids who use drugs will do drugs under almost any circumstances and will try anything they can find from drinking vanilla or lemon extract to eating nutmeg to get high. Girls have told of getting the children whom they babysat high and raiding medicine cabinets for any labeled or unlabeled pills while babysitting. Many kids admit to getting their pets high. They report use during scouting, church youth group, band and athletic activities. Some tell of getting high with their teachers, school counselors, therapists, policemen, probation officers. They use at school and on their jobs.

Vulnerable Situations: Parents need to be aware of the power of peer pressure. A child, and even an adult, will do things in a group that they would never do alone. An alert parent can avoid some situations which entail increased peer pressure, exposure to chemicals, or opportunities for deviant behavior. A telephone in a child's room allows unnecessary privacy. Even for the very young, sleep-overs provide opportunities for children to sneak out after the parents are asleep and vandalize or "party." Kids left alone at a shopping center have the opportunity to vandalize and shoplift, and are prey to drug dealers and child molesters. Rock concerts are known for prolific chemical use. Access to cars and empty homes during the day and evening provide safe places to do drugs.

Kids are especially vulnerable to peer pressure when they graduate from elementary to intermediate and then to high school. Each change brings new class structures, new freedoms, less supervision, and new or enlarged peer groups. Parents may be unaware of the change or expansion of a peer group. Loneliness and a desire to be part of a group can easily entice one into an undesirable peer group. Secrecy about friends is a danger signal.

It is very helpful to know the parents of a child's friends when deciding where and with whom the child will be allowed certain privileges. It is not unusual for families who have been accustomed to enjoying family activities with each other to find their philosophies on teenage supervision differ.

Learn to Seek Help: If parents do not feel good about their family relationships or their child's development, parenting classes, self help groups, or family therapy can be very helpful. A need for help is not a reflection of poor parenting, but is a ***positive*** message of care and concern. It is all right to seek help and learn from others.

Treatment Prevents the Spread of the Disease: One of the most frequent sources of first drug encounters is an older brother or sister. Placing a chemically dependent child in treatment is a very strong preventive measure for the other children in the family and their friends. It gives the children a strong "no use" message, and provides the help the family needs for its own recovery from this family disease.

Two of the Greatest Gifts You Can Give Your Children Are Roots and Wings.

WHAT ADOLESCENTS NEED

1. Limits set - What is safe and acceptable and what is not? Are consequences reasonable and consistent? Eliminate as much gray area as possible.
2. Fair and consistent discipline which carries over into every area of their lives.
3. Positive role models - How do you handle stress, celebration and social life?
4. The opportunity to honestly express their feelings and thoughts.
5. Nonacceptance of negative behavior. Acceptance of the child, tolerance for mistakes, and permission to fail and try again are essential.
6. The opportunity to laugh and an ability to enjoy "the.moment" when things go well.
7. Opportunities to be successful at home, in school and the community, and with peers. Encourage and boost all positive efforts of kids!
8. Structured family activities - church, meals, work, and recreation.
9. Consistency with friends, school policy, parents, rules and regulations.
10. Accurate information about alcohol and other drugs, crime, sexuality and other difficult areas.
11. Honest communication with parents and other adults.
12. Support from important adults in their lives and from peers.
13. To be trusted by important adults.
14. Genuine commitment from families and friends.
15. To be encouraged to be responsible.
16. To be respected. Treat them like you treat your closest friends.
17. To be touched. It is incredible that we need a bumper sticker to remind us to hug our kids!
18. LOVE. Have you told them you love them today?
19. A HIGHER POWER, as AA refers to IT. A Being greater than themselves to whom they can pray and ask for help.
20. YOU.

AN ADULT IS WHAT HAPPENS TO A CHILD!

Author Unknown

REFERENCES FOR PREVENTION IN THE FAMILY:
1, 2, 3, 6, 7, 8, 11, 39, 44, 50

5 PARENT GROUPS

Social changes occur because of citizen pressure and citizen commitment. Today citizen involvement is an essential ingredient of the solution to our nation's complicated drug problem. Drug traffickers will not experience meaningful consequences, laws will not be properly enforced, schools will not become drug free, treatment will not improve, and the media will not reverse its "do drug" messages until citizens present a united front and demand changes. The parent group movement provides a vehicle for citizens to organize and work together to prevent and reduce alcohol and other drug use, and to facilitate recovery of those who are chemically dependent. Three types of parent groups are discussed in this chapter:

1. Parent peer groups which focus on prevention and early intervention of chemical use through a close-knit parent support system;

2. Self-help support groups which provide care, support and tools of recovery for the loved ones of chemical users;

3. Community action groups which work to effect changes in the community.

THE BEGINNING OF THE MOVEMENT

The First Group: The first parent peer group began in 1976 when Dr. Marsha Manatt, an Atlanta mother and college professor, became alarmed upon discovering drug use among 12-14 year olds at her child's birthday party. Marsha assembled the parents of the children who attended the party. From that gathering evolved the first parent peer group. The parents set up guidelines for house rules and curfews and supported each other in enforcing codes of behavior they had established. The parents who stayed together and stuck to the plan saw their kids become drug free.

It Evolved into a Community Action Group: The discovery of the extent of drug use in adolescents, their own ignorance concerning drugs, the lack of good information available, and society's acceptance of drug use prompted them to become a community action group. Marsha wrote to Dr. Robert DuPont, the director of the National Institute on Drug Abuse at that time, and asked him for help. That plea led to contact with a local drug education expert, Dr. Thomas Gleaton, a Georgia State University professor. Gleaton and Manatt formed Parents Resource Institute of Drug Education (PRIDE) in 1977, which is still a major resource for other groups.

The Movement Spread Nationwide: By 1978, unknown to each other, parent groups were popping up all over the country. In 1980, the National Federation of Parents for Drug Free Youth (NFP) was founded to assist communities in forming groups and to serve as a networking resource for groups across the country. Networking groups were established in many states. Now there are approximately 9,000 parent groups in the U.S., most of which consist totally of volunteers. This movement is proving that parents can be effective and they do not have to be powerless over adolescent drug use.

PARENT PEER GROUPS

The Purpose Is Prevention and/or Early Intervention: As children enter junior high and high school their peer groups enlarge and extend beyond their immediate neighborhood. Parents usually are not acquainted with the parents of their children's new friends. They find themselves at a loss as children begin to claim "everyone does it" and ask for privileges that they say their friends have. Parents can build their own support system by forming a parent peer group with the parents of their children's friends. This can be an extremely effective method of preventing chemical use or "nipping it in the bud," if the children are in the early stage of use.

Description: A parent peer group consists of the parents of the children in a particular peer group. Parents become acquainted with one another and share their views on adolescent alcohol and drug use, discipline, house rules and responsibilities of the children in the peer group. They usually set up guidelines for rules and curfews (see Resource Section), support each other in the enforcement of each family's rules, and become well informed on the effects, signs and symptoms of alcohol and other drug use; work at family unity and improved communication within the family; and become more aware of the "do drug" messages with which our children are bombarded. With this type of parental support system children who have not started to experiment are less likely to begin and those who have started may stop if they are not yet chemically dependent.

Getting Started: If chemical use is suspected among the children, it might be more difficult to assemble the parents. They may already be experiencing a lot of pain and one can expect to find apathy, denial, defensiveness, and blame when making the calls for the first meeting. Do not tell parents that their child is doing drugs, but that you are concerned because there has been some drug use in your own child or in the group. Some parents will refuse to attend, some will come very reluctantly, while others may be grateful for the call and be ready to confront the problem. A non-blaming attitude is important. The first meeting should be a "parents only" meeting. It is best held in the home of someone who is very comfortable with the idea, or in a neutral place such as a church or school. Only two or three parents are needed to begin a group. Continue to contact those who do not attend on a periodic basis. As time passes they may become ready to share and enlist the help of a support group.

Accept Each Person Where They Are Today: If chemical use has already started in the children's peer group, some parents will have a lot of deep hurt, anger, fear, resentments, confusion, and perhaps conflict with a spouse to work through before they are able to build up trust in the group. People need their own time to work through negative feelings. Unconditional acceptance by the group hastens the process. For those who are able to overcome their difficulties and begin to work constructively with the group, there is a good chance the pay off will be alcohol and drug free-kids, and a close knit parent peer group. Children who do not become alcohol and drug-free despite such parental efforts may be chemically dependent and in need of professional treatment. Chemically dependent children whose parents have united and taken a strong stand are more likely to embrace treatment when they can no longer successfully manipulate their parents.

Meeting Format: After several getting acquainted meetings, the group may want to gain knowledge in some specific areas and invite guest speakers, attend parenting courses, or assign readings and reporting of pertinent literature. Another alternative is to model the meeting format after one of the self-help support groups or consider becoming a chapter of a national group.

SELF-HELP SUPPORT GROUPS

Purpose: Self-help support groups provide care, support, and tools for recovery for the loved ones of chemical users. These groups do not necessarily consist of the parents in the child's peer group, but are composed of people with similar problems.

Description: The groups usually have a structured format, follow strict rules of anonymity, and focus on personal change rather than attempting to change the user. Parents whose children are displaying behaviors which may be related to chemical use are welcome to these free meetings. Attendance at five or six meetings helps parents to determine if there is chemical use. If there is an alcohol or other drug problem, ongoing attendance will help parents learn how they enable their child's use and how to "let go" and allow the user to experience the consequences of his/her actions. Parents will learn how to work more constructively together. When these things begin to happen within the family, the user's games are no longer successful and recovery becomes attractive.

Examples: The national groups, Al-Anon, Nar-Anon, and Families Anonymous, are programs for the families and friends of alcohol and drug users. They are each based on the 12 steps of personal change of Alcoholics Anonymous (AA). Another national group is Toughlove. It is for parents who are experiencing any type of behavior problems with their children. Structured meetings give parents support in demanding responsible conduct from out-of-control family members.

Locating Groups: If phone numbers for these groups are not listed in the local phone book they may be available from the city or county agency for alcohol and other drug use, a mental health association, rehabilitation program, church, school, or hotline. Al-Anon groups are in most communities and often have a listed phone number. Families Anonymous, Nar-Anon, and Toughlove groups are not yet as numerous. They can be located, or new groups can be formed by contacting their national headquarters listed in the Resource Section.

COMMUNITY ACTION GROUPS

Community action groups are formed for many reasons. Groups get started when parents become alarmed about the easy availability of alcohol and other drugs in the community; because of a child's drug use; because a school principal asked some parents for help in dealing with the drug problem; because a community task force recommended it; or perhaps a fatal alcohol or drug related accident brought a family, school, or community leaders out of denial and into action. Parent peer groups often become community action groups. Action groups focus on educating themselves about alcohol and other drug use first, and then proceed to raise awareness in the community, refer families to treatment, reduce the availability of alcohol and other drugs, reverse "do-drug" media messages, and work on legislation. Schools are often their first target since children spend a large amount of their time in school and school related activities.

The remainder of this section tells the story of PANDAA (Parents' Association to Neutralize Drug and Alcohol Abuse, Inc.), and gives guidelines for starting a community action group and ideas for group actions.

There Is No End to the Good We Can Do
If We Don't Care Who Gets the Credit.

THE STORY OF PANDAA

PANDAA, (Parents' Association to Neutralize Drug and Alcohol Abuse, Inc.), is a parent group located in Fairfax County, Virginia, a large suburban community of 600,000 in the Washington, D.C. Metropolitan area. It is an affluent and transient area which has experienced rapid growth during the past 25 years. Fairfax County has a large school system which includes 24 high schools.

With my husband, Tom, I founded PANDAA in April 1980 because we were powerless over the alcohol and marijuana use of two of our children and we feared that the use would spread to our five other children. After encountering an attitude of denial among the parents of our children's friends and experiencing no success in curtailing the chemical use with family counseling and home remedies of discipline and curfews, we decided to approach our high school principal, Mr. Frank Elliott, with the parent group concept. The principal was very pleased to have someone willing to help him with a problem he openly admitted was out of hand. He suggested that the concept be presented to the Parent Teachers Organization (PTO) Board of Directors. The board voted that the group should be independent of the PTO, but agreed to finance a mailing of a notice for the first meeting. The letter stated statistics about drug abuse and presented possible actions that a parent group could undertake in our community. Of two intermediate schools that fed into the high school, one principal wholeheartedly supported a mailing to his student body while the other principal refused. The meeting notice was mailed to 2,000 families, and 120 people attended the first meeting.

The First Meeting: A recovering user who had attended our high school volunteered to speak and told of his alcohol and other drug use at school. His honesty and frankness jolted many people out of denial, but also created panic. Some parents threatened to remove their children from the school. There was fear among parents that people would think there was a drug problem in their family if they attended a meeting or if they signed up for a committee. At school there was much unrest and apprehension among the students and teachers. No one wanted their turf invaded. Despite the fears, denial, and anger, many people wanted to see changes made and signed up for committees.

Formal Structure Established: A steering committee was formed. The committee immediately began work on a name for the group, goals and by-laws. Within 6 weeks we had a name, a logo, a board of directors, by-laws, stationery and a membership form printed. We began collecting dues, opened a bank account, incorporated with nonprofit status, and purchased a nonprofit bulk mailing permit. Local politicians were contacted and were all very supportive.

Our Ignorance and Anger Were a Handicap: We soon realized we knew very little about the subject we were tackling. The term "responsible use" was new to us. We had to decide if we approved of adult responsible use of drugs or teenage responsible use of alcohol. We had to take a stand as a group. We began to educate ourselves. We learned about the drugs and their easy availability. As we began to understand that our children live in an environment quite different than the one we knew as adolescents, we felt less anger toward our children and the school personnel and became ready to do some constructive work.

The School Committee: The area of greatest concern was the school. At the school committee's first meeting there was a lot of anger and blame. We made no progress until we eliminated the blaming. Three people met with the principal and they learned what his problems and limitations were. He already had a plan for parents to assist with attendance record keeping, monitoring students leaving the school grounds during school hours, and recruiting more chaperones at dances. When school started in September, a plan was in place. It consisted mostly of strictly enforcing already existing rules plus a lot of visibility and volunteerism of parents. There were rumors of student rebellion, which never happened. The school atmosphere became orderly and much more conducive to learning. It was at least easier for non-users to stay straight.

Legislative Efforts: With the help of county politicians, we became involved in legislative efforts to pass a drug paraphernalia law and raise the drinking age. Through these activities we learned the legislative process, received important newspaper coverage, gained credibility, and met members of other parent groups in the state. Most important, we developed a new self-confidence that we could make a difference. Even though the bills were not passed that first year we learned that with perseverance they eventually get passed.

PANDAA Newsletter: We realized very soon that education of the public was a critical need. We held public awareness meetings and did extensive publicity for the meetings. The turnouts were very poor. Those who needed the information the most were not coming to awareness meetings. We began to publish an educational newsletter five times a year and sent it to all families in the school. Our principal allowed us to use the school's nonprofit bulk mailing permit until we were able to purchase our own. The newsletter was printed at cost in a community college print shop. It quickly became a very important instrument giving our group credibility, recognition, and a good reputation. After one year of free newsletters, many families sent in subscriptions allowing us to finance an expanded complimentary mailing list. Although there are only 300 paid subscriptions, we distribute locally and nationally 7,000 copies on a complimentary basis to schools, counselors, treatment programs, doctors, churches, libraries, law enforcement personnel, civic leaders, legislators, government agencies, awareness meetings and conferences. The newsletter has received national recognition.

A Media Project: In the spring of 1982, PANDAA became actively involved with an organized effort to convince a local radio station to discontinue the broadcast of an "adult" morning show which was extremely popular with teens and pre-teens. The disk jockey included a series of skits which condoned drug use and ridiculed religion and all forms of authority. The station ignored complaints, saying the show was not directed at children. The Federal Communications Commission (FCC) stated they could not help. We decided to contact the advertisers on the show. Along with a network of PTA and PTO volunteers, we monitored and taped the show for objectionable material and identified the advertisers. A mailing informed parents of the nature of the program and requested them to write to the companies which advertised on the show. Many of the companies responded that they had purchased advertising through an agency, were unaware of the type of show selected for their advertising, and proceeded to cancel their contract. The show was removed from the air.

A Treatment Program Comes to Our Community: As we worked in our schools and community we realized that this work was not "fixing" the children who were already chemically dependent. More families began to place their children into treatment. But for too many the results were unsatisfactory. We found a long term, intensive program in Florida which was experiencing good success rates. As families traveled the 800 miles to the Florida program, their enthusiastic stories about the dramatic changes in their children spread rapidly and each week new families took the long journey. They began to organize to bring a branch of the program to our community. In November, 1982, after a year and a half, the dream was realized. One hundred families who could not tolerate seeing their children destroyed by chemical use had joined together, raised funds, searched for a building, weathered zoning battles, and completely renovated the facility by themselves. Hundreds of young people have graduated from the program. They and their parents have spread much awareness throughout our community and have contributed to this book. Some of the parents have made career changes and are now working in the addiction field.

Court Watch: In October 1982, a Court Watch committee was formed. Volunteers observed trials and sentencings of drug cases in the Circuit Court and recorded all pertinent observations. The statistics were printed in the PANDAA newsletter and sent as a news release to over 150 resources including the media, judges, legislators and other interested persons. In the beginning, our focus was almost entirely on gathering information regarding the length of sentence imposed upon convicted drug dealers. After we learned the system and persistently followed-up on other observations we had made we were able to effect many changes. Jail times have been increased. Laws regarding convicted aliens are better enforced.

Victim Impact Statements have been filed which influenced judges to give long-term sentences to several big time marijuana dealers. Legislation has been enacted.

Anti-drug Program Initiated in the School System: As our children went into treatment, they began to tell us of their drug use at school. We learned that alcohol and other drug use was rampant during school hours, in sports, and in every other school-related activity. The work we had done in our local school was merely a band-aid. We realized that we had to approach the school superintendent because the rules were weak and school principals were not always receiving support from their superiors when they attempted to enforce rules. In March of 1983, thirty-six parents and recovering kids met with the superintendent and told their stories. He appointed a task force which met for several months, and then drew up recommendations which became school policy. Strong regulations aimed at precipitating families into treatment were passed by the school board nine months after our first meeting with the superintendent and almost four years after PANDAA's founding. The program was presented at the White House and Mrs. Nancy Reagan lauded it as a national model. Three semesters after the new, tougher policies were enacted substance abuse violations decreased from over 1100 per year to less than 500 per year.

Listening Ear Service: Still filled with painful memories of feeling alone and being afraid to verbalize suspected usage, parents of recovering children expressed a desire to help parents who were experiencing problems. A listening ear service was started in November 1983 with 15 volunteer parents whose children had completed treatment. A phone with a call forwarding system was installed in a parent's home. The phone number of the volunteer for the day is call-forwarded to her home. A manual was written for the personnel. Free informational material is provided for the callers.

Mocktail Dance: PANDAA has sponsored two adult alcohol-free dances with big band music. It gives parents a chance to show kids that they can have a good time without alcohol, and serves as a fundraising event.

Youth Group: In 1987 and 1988, a busload of students and teachers attended the PRIDE Conference in Atlanta under the sponsorship of PANDAA and our local Elks Lodge. Students received leadership training to help them start alcohol and drug-free youth groups in their schools.

Fundraising: Our major expenses are the publication of our newsletter, postage, and telephone expenses. Our volunteers are reimbursed for travel, postage and office expenses. Our principal source of funding is the 300 paid subscription fees to the newsletter, which are often accompanied by small donations of $5 to $20. We receive occasional donations of $100 to $1000 from service clubs, churches, or individuals. A $5,000 grant from the Junior League of Northern Virginia financed the production costs and the first printing of this book.

These are some of the major accomplishments of PANDAA. Most have been done by only a handful of people. Media publicity, professional looking stationery, and a regular newsletter have portrayed us as a large influential group. In reality we are a tiny influential group, with a few people who have persevered sometimes for a number of years to see a goal achieved. Many times we thought we were at a standstill only to find six months later that we had made many ripples of which we were not aware. We have learned not to give up.

GETTING A GROUP STARTED

Advance Work For The First Meeting

Some things can be done ahead of time, which will facilitate a smoother start, help curtail negative emotions, especially anger and blame and will set a tone of positive attitudes. If the leader can display some knowledge and obvious efforts of research at the first meeting, people are more likely to believe it will be worthwhile to participate in the efforts.

Find Support in the Community: Be positive. Without accusing people of doing a poor job or of rampant drug use in their facility, contact various factions of the professional community and ask for help and public support of the parent group or task force concept. If an early contact refuses support, make another visit after support has been gained from other professionals. Persons whose support can be very important include school administrators, PTA's, the police department, narcotics officers, the sheriff, the commonwealth or district attorney, elected officials, the city or county agency for substance abuse, private rehabilitation programs, pediatricians, and the clergy. Don't forget that most of these people are parents too! It is preferable to have two people make the visits together.

Publicity: The professionals whose support has been gained may help with publicity. They may allow use of mailing lists, copying or printing resources, do press releases, or announce meetings in their newsletter and bulletins. Press releases can be sent to newspapers, radio, and TV and flyers can be posted in shopping centers and distributed door to door in neighborhoods.

Define the Problem: The existence of 9,000 parent groups across the nation demonstrates the prevalence of the problem in all types of communities. Gather national statistics, drug information, and success stories of other communities from the sources listed in the Resource Section. Assemble evidence that there is a problem in your local community. Inquire if there have been state, county, or school surveys. Talk to school personnel, youth leaders, counselors, and law enforcement personnel, especially the officer on the street. Attend an open Alcoholics Anonymous (AA) or Narcotics Anonymous (NA) meeting, or visit other rehabilitation programs to hear users' testimonials. Consider asking a recovering user to speak at a meeting.

Demonstrate the Availability of Alcohol and Drugs: Watch for young people purchasing alcohol at convenience stores. Ask kids at AA or NA meetings how they obtained alcohol and drugs. Collect newspaper articles and other media reports.

Demonstrate the Media's "Do Drugs" Messages: Collect a list of movies, TV shows, music lyrics, and commercial products with pro-drug messages such as OPIUM perfume. Collect pro-drug editorial articles in the newspapers. Attend a rock concert and witness the blatant alcohol and drug use and the management's and local police department's acceptance of it.

Learn about the Legal System: Become aware of the court system's handling of drug cases. Attend some sentencings and trials of drug felony cases and note the sentences given. Do they reflect the severity of the crime?

Provide Hope: Many parents attend meetings hoping to find help for their child. Collect information on local self-help groups and treatment programs and compile a referral list. The city or county agency for alcohol and other drug use can provide this information.

Gather Informational Materials for Distribution: The supportive professionals may provide some materials. Read all literature and check for "responsible use," and pro-drug messages before distributing. See the Resource Section for good literature and tips on evaluating literature.

The First Meeting

Be Patient - Understand Where People Are Coming From: Many strong feelings may surface since alcohol and drug use is a very personal, emotional, volatile and threatening subject. Some people will be fearful of the stigma they think will be attached to participation in this type of group. Some will be filled with anger and blame. Perhaps they have already lost children. Others will totally deny that there is any problem in the school or community. Many will expect instant solutions. Some may be so upset about their own child that they are unable to contribute to the group at this time, or they may unrealistically believe that taking part in the group will cure their child's alcohol and other drug use. Attending this public meeting may be a giant step for a parent just coming out of denial. Despite negative feelings, there will be some who are ready, willing and able to contribute.

Replace Guilt with Hope: Make it clear that children begin using alcohol and other drugs because of peer pressure, curiosity, and easy availability, not because of poor parenting. Stress that these children are not "bad" but have become sick and need help. Give parents hope that there is help available for drug-involved children. Explain the parent peer group concept and provide literature on AA, Al-Anon, other self-help groups in the community and treatment programs.

Begin with a Non-blaming, Non-threatening Attitude: Demonstrate that the school, police, court system or politicians cannot solve the problem alone. A self-righteous attitude is counter-productive. Learn what the problems of each agency are and then assist them and give them support when possible.

Will This Involvement Embarrass My Children? Involvement is one of the strongest messages of care a parent can give to a straight or using child. A straight child who cannot handle the embarrassment of a parent's involvement of this sort is a candidate for future use. Parental involvement gives high risk children a strong positive message. While children make their own choice about chemical use, parents can choose to strive for a safer environment for their children. If a child is in the early stages of use, parental involvement may assist recovery of the user. On the other hand, parental involvement might precipitate an increase in drug use because the child is already chemically dependent and is in need of professional treatment.

Parents of Non-users: Parents must realize the tremendous impact other children's drug use has on straight children. The behavior of a drug-using child in the classroom disrupts the learning of all children. The teacher no longer has control of the classroom, just as the parent of an abuser no longer has control of the family. The same disruptive process occurs when there are alcohol and other drug users on a team or in a band or club. Chemical use and its accompanying rebellious attitudes are contagious, and use by a few members of a closely knit team or club can spread like wildfire.

Set Date for a Second Meeting: Give parents examples of successful actions taken in other communities. Demonstrate some possibilities for your community. Do not leave the first meeting without setting a date for the next meeting and compiling a list of people who want to be called and reminded of the next meeting. Provide sign-up sheets for committees. A steering committee is essential. Don't be disappointed if only five or ten people come to the first meeting. If just three or four become active participants incredible things can be accomplished.

The Basics

Become Official: Decide if the group will be a PTA committee or if it would like to be an independent entity. A name, board of directors, by-laws, logo, printed stationery, and a bank account gives group members a sense of commitment, unity, purpose, and a feeling of permanence. To the public it transmits knowledge, credibility, authority, stability and power. Official status also provides a base for soliciting donations from businesses and service clubs. It enables one to secure locations for programs and enlist the help of other groups. Many people are reluctant to solicit membership dues when they form a group. Businesses and citizens are more likely to contribute if there is a formal structure and a service is performed such as awareness meetings, distribution of educational materials, or publication of a newsletter.

Board of Directors: A board of directors may evolve from a steering committee. If public officials or professionals are considered for the board, determine that they have enough interest and time to attend regular meetings. It may be more desirable to invite them to be members of an advisory board.

By-laws and Tax Exempt Status: When writing by-laws, consider that the group will probably be a small core group of workers with limited time. Keep things simple, such as size of board, length of office, frequency of required meetings, duties of officers and election requirements. Study by-laws of other nonprofit tax exempt volunteer groups, such as the local PTA. Write by-laws in language that will be acceptable for gaining nonprofit status from the IRS. Forms and instructions for application can be obtained from the IRS. ***It is a simple procedure.*** Incorporating the group is not necessary to obtain nonprofit status, although there are definite advantages to incorporating. When nonprofit tax-free status is acheived, tax-free donations can be solicited, applying for funding will be facilitated and a nonprofit bulk mailing permit can be purchased from the U.S. Postal Service. A nonprofit bulk mailing permit allows a large discount for mailings of 200 pieces or more.

Get Educated and Take a Stand: After members have become reasonably knowledgeable about the many aspects of alcohol and other drug use, consider composing a statement of philosophy which includes controversial questions sometimes asked in public. Some of these issues are: responsible adult use of drugs, responsible use of alcohol by underage adolescents, the legalization of drugs, the disease concept of chemical dependency, and use of mind-altering prescription drugs in treatment. (See **PANDAA Philosophies** in Resource Section.)

Stay Apolitical: Don't allow the group to be used for the purposes of a particular political party by supporting the election of a candidate.

Chemical use is a bipartisan issue. The group's volunteerism and apolitical stand gives it a unique power and influence that other factions don't have.

Media Publicity: Make considerable efforts to get media coverage of all group meetings and activities. Positive media publicity is an extremely powerful force. It makes one an instant authority on the subject, whether or not that status is deserved. Before seeking publicity, get informed. If invited to be on a panel, ask who the other speakers are. It is not advisable to be on a panel or program debating with a pro-drug advocate. Avoid being a guest on a call-in radio or TV show until you feel confident that you can give good answers to the pro-drug call-ins. ***It requires a lot of experience and knowledge to refute the convincing arguments of pro-drug advocates.*** Be careful of providing them an opportunity for publicity at your expense.

Meetings with Public Officials and Professionals: When meeting with officials such as a school principal or superintendent, police chief, etc. always go with at least one other person. Begin with a non-threatening, non-blaming attitude. Learn the official's side of the problem and offer help and support. Be aware that there are many laws that restrict them from doing what they really would like to do. Have notes prepared, and record notes during the meeting. Be up-front and honest. If the results of the meeting will be publicized, allow the official an opportunity to edit or clarify the write-up.

Fundraising and Cost Cutting: Besides collecting dues, soliciting donations, having bake sales, etc., funds can be realized in the form of free services or services done at cost. Some large businesses have their own print shop and will print material free with credit given. Print shops in high schools or community colleges may print free or at cost. Churches, schools, or public officials may allow use of their copy machine. A school, PTA, or county agency may sponsor a mailing using their nonprofit bulk mailing permit. A state agency may have films, literature, and grants available for prevention work. Service clubs are good resources for funding. The national organizations of the Lions, the Elks, the Optimists and the Kiwanis have adopted substance abuse as one of their priorities. In many communities, the Junior League has become involved in this issue.

Start With Small Projects

Work for One Success at a Time: The choice of projects will depend on the talents available in the group. It may be best to start with small, non-threatening projects, such as awareness meetings, lobbying for legislation, a parent pledge campaign, etc. Before tackling a big project like bringing a school system out of deep denial, it may be best to first build up credibility, establish a reputation, prove the permanence and commitment of the group, and get acquainted with all factions of the community which might assist in the big project. If an undertaking is not fruitful, don't give up, the community may be ready for it at a later date. Each project has an impact somewhere, whether or not it is obvious. Go on to other projects and strive for a steady pace of activity.

Parent Pledge Campaign: A good first project for a group is a parent pledge campaign. Junior high school is not too early to start. Parents are asked to sign a pledge that they will not serve alcohol to individuals under 21 years in their home and all parties in their home for school age children will be chaperoned and will be free of alcohol and other drugs. The pledge is published in the PTA or principal's newsletter, and/or in a local newspaper. Parents send in their pledges and they are kept on file. A number is provided for parents to call and check to see if the host of a party their child has been invited to has signed the pledge. To increase its impact public support of the pledge can be solicited from the school board, county government, police department, etc. A sample parent pledge is in the Resource Section.

Red Ribbon Campaign: The displaying of red ribbons to signify a commitment to the war on drugs is a nationwide movement. A campaign can be done in the same manner as, or in combination, with a parent pledge campaign. Distribution of red ribbons at awareness meetings, church gatherings, social gatherings, etc. are a good non-threatening way of bringing the drug issue out in the open. The National Federation of Parents (NFP) sponsors a National Red Ribbon Week during the month of October. Special red ribbons can be purchased from the NFP or red ribbon can be bought in a fabric store.

Letter Writing and Phone Calling: Some groups spend the first part of every meeting writing letters. One letter or call represents 400 citizens. Letters and calls are crucial tools for bringing about changes and legislation in local, state, and national governments. Ask your county agencies to inform you when you can help them through calls and letters to obtain funding they need for alcohol and drug services. In some instances the effectiveness of writing increases if copies are sent to the official's peers, superiors, and other pertinent parties. Indicate at the bottom of the letter, to whom copies were sent. Letters are also a very important vehicle for reversing the media's do drug messages. Letters to the editor are very effective. A telephone tree for recruiting callers and writers on urgent issues is very valuable. Tips for letter writing and addresses of TV Networks are in the Resource Section.

Awareness Programs for Parents: Parents seem to know less about drugs than the kids. Parents need more information on the drug culture and the signs and symptoms of use than the pharmacological effects of drugs. It is not advisable to have parents and children attend awareness programs together. Some of the information parents need is not appropriate for the children. After becoming informed, parents can select the information they want their children to have and share it with them personally.

A program may vary according to the group of parents being addressed. If it is for parents of high school age children, some will already have children who are chemically dependent, and more emphasis will be needed on relieving guilt and anger, the disease concept of chemical use, and help that is available.

It is sometimes easier to attract parents of grade school and junior high school children to a meeting because they are not as threatened by the sometimes imagined stigma attached to attendance at this type of meeting. They are the optimum target for prevention.

A testimonial by a recovering user or the parent of a user will surpass almost any other type of presentation. The police department will usually provide a policeman to speak and a drug paraphernalia display. An informed parent can give a very adequate presentation. Other speaker possibilities are personnel from a rehabilitation program or county agency, a judge, an undercover agent, etc. There are also good films available (see Resource Section for sources). Schedule no more than one or two speakers or films in an evening. Time left for questions is very important. Some groups do a series of meetings on parenting techniques with appropriate guest speakers. Topics to cover are:

1. Explain the availability of alcohol and drugs, the "do drug" messages, and the reasons kids do drugs.
2. Relieve guilt, assuring parents they are not the cause of a child's use.
3. Explain the increased potency of marijuana, its slow excretion rate, and its fat solubility characteristics, which cause it to be deposited in the brain. Pot's anti-nausea property encourages the intake of large amounts of alcohol.
4. Give alcohol equal time, stressing it causes the same behavior problems as other drugs. Discuss responsible use issue.
5. Show drug paraphernalia which can be obtained from the police department.
6. Teach the signs and symptoms of use emphasizing that they are usually not recognized until usage has been ongoing for 1 to 2 years.
7. Teach disease concept of chemical use.
8. Give hope - treatment is available.

Education of the Professional Community: Because so many professionals have not been trained in the diagnosis and treatment of chemical dependency, many children are misdiagnosed at least once before the proper diagnosis is made. Many doctors believe it is unethical to reveal the results of urine testing to parents even though they would not hesitate to reveal the results of any other testing to parents. Some professionals still believe in responsible use, that chemical use is a symptom of other problems, that drug users can use alcohol, that alcoholics can use drugs, and do not expect total abstinence from their clients. Some agencies still distribute responsible use literature.

Parent groups can make presentations to the various professional groups. It is wise for group members to seek board positions on the city or county agencies, committees and task forces. In these groups you will get a pulsebeat of the community and its extent of denial, have an opportunity to educate and express your philosophies, and build a precious network of supporters.

Facilitate the Establishment of Self-Help Support Groups: These free support groups offer immediate help and comfort to people in severe pain.

Distribution of Literature: Check school libraries for pro-drug literature. Ask book stores to sell accurate literature. Distribute literature to public and school libraries, churches, stores, etc.

Newsletter: The written word is one of the most powerful tools available. A newsletter can serve as an educational service, a legislative tool, a networking agent, a brochure, and a tool to gain credibility, authority, and a reputation. It can be a means of educating the counseling, medical, education, and legal professions if they are included in the mailing list.

The frequency and size of publication depends on the editor's experience and time available, and the funds provided. A larger, less frequent publication might be more effective and cheaper to produce and mail than a smaller monthly publication. The per-copy cost decreases as the number of copies printed increases. A very large printing of one yearly issue can be distributed throughout the year at awareness meetings etc. When planning a newsletter consult with the printer to learn the cheapest format for production. To save on paper and mailing costs, a camera ready copy can be typed and laid out on oversize paper. At no extra cost the printer can reduce the size of the print giving 30-50% more material on a page.

Legislation: A group must first get an idea of what bills it would like to support. Acquire the legislative packet of such groups as PTA, the school system, the police department, the county treatment agency, and the district or commonwealth attorney. From these, the group can pick bills it would like to support or oppose, or it may decide it wants a bill not listed in any of the packets.

Legislators are not influenced by citizens outside their own jurisdiction. To get a bill introduced and passed, it is vital to have contact with groups throughout the state who will contact their particular legislators. Coordinate with other parent groups in the state. Other groups sensitive to substance abuse may be the PTA, associations for teachers, school principals, police, doctors, wives of doctors, women's clubs, service clubs, treatment facilities, county and state agencies, etc. Many of these groups have state networks and are politically active.

To get a bill introduced in the state legislature it is best to have multiple sponsors who have considerable influence. The bill must then pass through its assigned study committee. Support is needed from the constituents of each legislator on that committee. If it is approved by the study committee, it goes to the floor and needs support from the constituents of all legislators. Contact with groups throughout the state can bring support for each step of the way. Don't give up, it often takes 2 or 3 years to get a bill passed.

Laws that might interest a group are: Civil forfeiture (seizure of assets gained from illegal drug distribution), immunity against civil suit for school personnel reporting suspected substance abuse, mandatory reporting of substance abuse by school personnel, drug free school zone areas, revocation of driver's license for drug offenders, stronger drug trafficking laws, and mandatory jail sentencing for drug trafficking. The U.S. Department of Justice has a model bill for states to use for drafting civil forfeiture laws.

Court Watch: Court Watch is a good early activity for a parent group because it requires no previous knowledge or experience. It is one of the best ways of learning what is actually happening on the legal end of substance abuse, and it can be done with only a few volunteers. Volunteers observe trials and sentencings of drug related cases and record their observations. The statistics can be used to apply pressure for stronger sentencing of drug felony cases, for improving record keeping methods in the judicial system, and in many other ways. The **COURTS AND DRUGS** book listed on page 126 recounts court watching experiences of PANDAA, suggestions for starting a Court Watch program and provides forms for recording statistics.

Big Projects

The School System and Drugs: School principals and superintendents use the same denial and enabling systems and experience the same feelings of guilt and failure as parents when it comes to drug problems. Until those obstacles are overcome, an effective and comprehensive program will not be initiated. A school principal is powerless until there is full support of the superintendent of schools. Drug education will not have an effect until students observe that adults are concerned enough about the effects of drugs to give strong consequences for use and to require treatment of students diagnosed as chemically dependent. A parent group and school personnel need a lot of education, commitment, and support of each other to establish a program that will do these things. Handbooks listed in the Resource

Section, page 110, give suggestions for initiating a school program and examples of school regulations which have brought about positive changes.

Drug-Free Youth Groups: A youth group promoting an alcohol and drug free life style can be a very powerful means of reversing peer pressure. Before undertaking the sponsorship of such a group, parents or school personnel should first be very aware and able to identify chemical use, and be certain that the group maintains a "no use" philosophy rather than a "responsible use" philosophy. The responsible use philosophy implies that it is all right for adolescents to drink if they don't drive. Parents and school personnel often embrace the responsible use belief rationalizing that "at least it's a step in the right direction and it is saving lives." In reality it is another adult giving mixed messages and condoning health damaging, illegal practices. The NFP, PRIDE and Youth to Youth have manuals and offer training workshops for youth group leaders which follow the no use philosophy. (See Resource Section.)

Implementing Changes in Government Agencies: Learning the system, laying careful groundwork, networking, diplomacy, patience, and a lot of time (often several years) are necessary to effect changes in systems which are dependent on public funding and bogged down with bureaucracy. Attitudes and philosophies of many people may have to be changed. Budgeting allowances for desired changes have to be planned one to two years in advance. A parent group's history of being apolitical and volunteer can give it added influence. Letter writing campaigns, speaking at public hearings, and getting a member on a committee or task force responsible for the particular system, support from both political parties and media involvement are all helpful tools.

Community Intervention: One of the major stumbling blocks of progress is turf protection among school personnel, the police department, the probation department, the court system, social workers, treatment personnel, etc. Each tend to stay in their own little niche and avoid communicating with each other. They often blame each other, rather than attempting to learn about each others' problems and to devise methods to help each other to better serve the community. A process called community intervention can solve this problem. This can be a very extensive but rewarding project for a parent group to undertake. Participation is solicited from leaders of all factions of the community who have occasion to deal with alcohol and other drug use in some form. A professional facilitator educates all persons on all aspects of the problem so they each begin to see all sides of the problem, rather than their own specialized area. As they all begin to communicate, each agency learns how to improve their own services, eliminate duplication of efforts, and begin to work more effectively with each other.

REFERENCES FOR THIS CHAPTER: 1, 3, 5, 51

SUMMING IT UP

Adolescent chemical use is a new phenomenon which has developed over the past 25 years. Since the first generation of adolescent users has joined the work force, it has become clear that we can no longer consider adolescent chemical use as a harmless phase that most kids go through. Too many adolescent users continue use in adulthood. The government, the military, professional sports, and private industry have been forced to focus on the problem of alcohol and drugs in the workplace because chemical use is affecting job performance. These are signs of the disease stage of chemical use. Chemical use must be recognized as a health and safety issue not a rights, privacy, or personal choice issue.

Early symptoms of adolescent chemical use are not easily detected, few experts recognize the disease, and there is fear, embarassment, shame, rejection and hopelessness associated with a positive diagnosis. Consequently, it seems easier to those involved to deny the problem rather than to face it, despite the fact that they are experiencing excrutiating emotional pain. When the disease comes out of the closet and becomes an acceptable disease that can be talked about, more families will enter treatment. Treatment must be improved and become more available and affordable. Because chemical dependency is a "contagious disease," treatment is a key factor in preventing its spread.

The rising death rate of the age group 15 to 24 years, the high school drop out rate, teenage pregnancy, and the rising crime rate are all closely associated with alcohol and drug use. A study done in the Fairfax County, Virginia jail revealed that 95% of the inmates were under the influence of alcohol and/or drugs at the time of their arrest. Crimes committed by users affect everyone in the community. Citizens must begin to recognize the impact chemical use is having in their local communities and on our country.

We do not have to allow chemical use to destroy our families and our country. It is our choice to take action. We can learn how to strengthen our families from within and reach out into our communities to reverse the many factors that nurture chemical use. There are already many grass-roots parent groups across the country fighting the war on drugs. They are helping families to help themselves and they are mobilizing their communities. We need more groups in more communities.

Along with drug education, schools must adapt and enforce strict rules concerning use. The entertainment industry and the media must reverse its "do drugs" messages. Society must consider chemical use unacceptable. Our courts must take a hard line on drug trafficking, and strong laws must be passed and enforced. Adults have a responsibility to be good role models to our youth.

It is up to each and every one of us to do our part to make these things happen. They will not happen unless citizens demand it. Each little action in the school, church, or community produces many ripples. A handful of volunteers can change an entire community.

REFERENCES

1. Macdonald, Donald, M.D., **Drugs, Drinking and Adolescents,** Year Book Medical Publishers, Chicago, 1984.
2. DuPont, Robert L., Jr., M.D., **Getting Tough on Gateway Drugs**, American Psychiatric Press, Inc., Washington, D.C., 1984.
3. Manatt, Marsha, Ph.D., **Parents, Peers and Pot**, DHEW Pub. No. (ADM) 79-8120, U.S. Government Printing Office, Washington, D.C., 1979.
4. **Potency Monitoring Project, Research Institute of Pharmaceutical Sciences**, School of Pharmacy, University of Mississippi. Project of NIDA, 1988.
5. Mann, Peggy, **Marijuana Alert**, McGraw-Hill Book Co., New York, 1985.
6. Adams, Ronald D., Ed.D., and Gleaton, Thomas J., Ed.D., **The PRIDE Questionnaire National Summary Data Report, 1987-88**, National Parents' Resource Institute for Drug Education, Inc., Atlanta, 1988.
7. The Media-Advertising Partnership for a Drug-Free America, Inc., **The Attitudinal Basis of Drug Use - 1987 and Changing Attitudes Toward Drug Use - 1988**, Gordon S. Black Corporation, Rochester, NY, 1988.
8. Polson, Beth, and Newton, Miller, Ph.D., **Not My Kid**, Arbor House, New York, 1984.
9. Johnson, Vernon E., **Intervention: How to Help Someone Who Doesn't Want Help**, Johnson Institute Books, Minneapolis, MN, 1986.
10. Johnson, Vernon E., **I'll Quit Tomorrow**, Harper and Row, New York, 1973.
11. Wilmes, David J., **Parenting for Prevention: How to Raise a Child to Say No to Alcohol/Drugs**, Johnson Institute Books, Minneapolis, MN, 1988.
12. Schaefer, Dick, **Choices & Consequences: What to Do When a Teenager Uses Alcohol/Drugs**, Johnson Institute Books, Minneapolis, MN, 1987.
13. Dickert, Gale D., **The Family Connection: A Guidebook for Florida Families**, pg. 93-97, Code 10, Inc., Perry, FL, 1988.
14. Pickens, Roy W., Ph.D., and Svikis, Dace S., B.A., **Biological Vulnerability to Drug Abuse**, NIDA Research Monograph 89, DHHS Pub. No. (ADM) 88-1590, U.S. Government Printing Office, Washington, D.C., 1988.
15. Wegscheider, Sharon, **Another Chance: Hope & Health for the Alcoholic Family**, Science and Behavior Books, Inc., Palo Alto, CA., 1981.
16. Tennant, Forest S., M.D., Dr. P.H., **Rapid Eye Test to Detect Drug Influence**, Veract, Inc., West Covina, CA, 1987.
17. Milam, James, M.D., and Ketcham, Katherine, **Under the Influence**, Bantam Books, New York, 1981.
18. Voth, Harold, M.D., **Marijuana and Effects on Young Adults,** Paper presented at New York University Medical School, June 29, 1979, New York City, for the Second Annual Conference on Marijuana.

19. National Institute on Alcohol Abuse and Alcoholism, "Physiological Effects of Alcohol," **Alcohol Topics IN BRIEF**, February, 1982, National Clearinghouse for Alcohol Information, Rockville, MD.

20. Mann, Peggy, **Arrive Alive**, Woodmere Press, New York, 1983.

21. Eckardt, Michael J., Ph.D., Harford, Thomas C., Ph.D., et al., "Health Hazards Associated with Alcohol Consumption," **Journal American Medical Association**, Vol 246:648-666, 1981

22. Senior, John R., M.D., Redeker, Allan G., M.D., Maddrey, Willis C., M.D., and Galambos, John T., M.D.; **Alcoholic Hepatitis A Practical Guide for Physicians and Other Health Care Professionals**, DHHS Pub. No. (ADM) 88-1549, U.S. Government Printing Office, Washington, D.C., 1988.

23. Valles, Jorge, M.D., **From Social Drinking to Alcoholism**, Tane Press, Dallas, TX, 1969.

24. U.S. Dept. of Health and Human Services, **The Fifth Special Report to the U.S. Congress on Alcohol and Health from the Secretary of Health and Human Services - December 1983**, DHHS Pub. No. (ADM) 84-1291, U.S. Government Printing Office, Washington, D.C.

25. O'Brien, Robert, and Chafetz, Morris, M.D. (Eds.), The **Encyclopedia of Alcoholism**, New York, Facts on File Publications, 1982.

26. Klonoff, H., 1974, "Marijuana and Driving in Real-Life Situations," **Science** 186: 317-324.

27. Mann, Peggy, "Marijuana Update," **Reader's Digest** Reprints, 1979 & 1980.

28. Russel, George K., **Marihuana Today**, Myrin Institute, New York, 1980.

29. Heath, Robert G., **Marijuana and the Brain**, The American Council on Marijuana and Other Psychoactive Drugs, Inc., 1981.

30. Gilkeson, Robert C., M.D., "Marijuana: Toxic to Cells," **Drug Awareness Information Newsletter**, October, 1987.

31. U.S. Department of Health and Human Services, **Drug Abuse and Drug Abuse Research - The Second Triennial Report to Congress**, DHHS Pub. No. (ADM) 87-1486, U.S. Government Printing Office, Washington, D.C., 1987.

32. U.S. Department of Health and Human Services, "Marijuana Smoking Style Increases Lung Effects and Cancer Risk," "High Prolactin Levels Seen in Cocaine Addicts During Treatment," "Medical Facets of Cocaine Abuse," "Mother's Drug Use Affects Infant Immune System," "Infant Stools Reveal Mother's Drug Use," **NIDA Notes**, Summer 1988, DHHS Pub. No. (ADM) 88-1488.

33. U. S. Dept of Justice, Drug Enforcement Administration, **Drugs of Abuse**, Government Printing Office, Washington, D.C., 1985-482-711.

34. Johnson, N. Peter, Ph.D., **Third Edition - Dictionary of Street Alcohol and Drug Terms**, School of Medicine University South Carolina, Columbia, SC, 1988.

35. Gold, Mark, M.D., 800 - **COCAINE**, Bantam Books, New York, 1984,

36. Chatlos, Calvin, M.D., **CRACK: What You Should Know about the Cocaine Epidemic**, Perigee Books, New York, 1987.

37. Rusche, Sue, **CRACK UPDATE**, Families in Action National Drug Information Center, Atlanta, 1986.

38. U.S. Department of Health and Human Services, "Crack Smokers More Violent and Psychotic Than Other Cocaine Users," "Drugged in the Womb: What Harm to Babies?" **NIDA Notes**, Winter 1987/88, DHHS Pub. No. (ADM) 88-1488.

39. U.S. Department of Health and Human Services, **The Health Consequences of Smoking, Nicotine Addiction, a Report of the Surgeon General**, DHHS Pub. No. (CDC) 88-8406, U.S. Government Printing Office, Washington, D.C., 1988.

40. U.S. Department of Health and Human Services, "Smokeless Tobacco: A Health Risk to Adolescents," and "Designer Drugs: A New Concern for the Drug Abuse Community," **NIDA NOTES**, December, 1985, U.S. Government Printing Office, Washington, D.C., 1985-491-332-20536.

41. Krug, Elsie, R.N. & McGuigan, Hugh, Ph.D., M.D., **Pharmacology in Nursing**, pg. 291-296, 312-313, 404-406, C.V. Mosby Co., St. Louis, 1955.

42. Wells, Susan, J., Ph.D., "Caffeine: Implications of Recent Research for Clinical Practice," **American Journal Orthopsychiatry**, 54 (3), July 1984 pg. 375-389.

43. Clouet, Doris, H., Ph.D., **Phencyclidine: an Update**, NIDA Research Monograph 64, DHHS Pub. No. (ADM) 86-1443, U.S. Government Printing Office, Washington, D.C., 1986.

44. Johnston, L.D., O'Malley, P.M., and Bachman, J.G., **Illicit Drug Use, Smoking, and Drinking by American High School Students, College Students, and Young Adults - 1975-1987**, DHHS Pub. No. (ADM) 89-1602, U.S. Government Printing Office, Washington, D.C., 1989.

45. Schwartz, Richard H., M.D., "When to Suspect Inhalant Abuse," **Patient Care**, May 30, 1989.

46. Shafer, Jack, "Designer Drugs," **Science**, March 85, Vol. 6 (2).

47. Cohen, Sidney, M.D., "Over-the-Counter Medicines: Psychophysiologic Reactions," **Drug Abuse & Alcoholism Newsletter**, Vol. IX, No. 7, September 1980.

48. "Clove Cigarettes Dangers," **Listen Magazine**, March, 1985.

49. Tennant, Forest S., M.D., Dr. P.H., **Anabolic Steroids**, Veract, Inc., Covina, CA, 1987.

50. Borton, Terry, Ed.D, Johnson and Lynell, Ph.D, **The *Weekly Reader* National Survey on Drugs and Drinking**, Field Publications, Middletown, CT, 1987.

51. Manatt, Marsha, Ph.D., **Parents, Peers and Pot II**, DHHS Pub. No. (ADM) 83-1290, U.S. Government Printing Office, Washington, D.C., 1983.

RESOURCE SECTION

READING LIST

Getting Tough On Gateway Drugs,[2,3,5] Robert DuPont, Jr., M.D., 1984, 330 pages. Presents the drug problem, the drug dependence syndrome, the gateway drugs (alcohol, marijuana, and cocaine), and how families can prevent and treat drug problems. This psychiatrist gives parents excellent support in implementing tough love techniques for users under and over 18 years. American Psychiatric Press, Inc., Washington, D.C. ISBN 0-88048-046-7, $7.95.

Drugs, Drinking and Adolescents, Donald I. Macdonald, M.D., 1984, 200 pages. Describes the stages of drug involvement, the drugs, diagnosis and treatment. The pediatrician author, who experienced the problem in his own family, addresses professionals and parents. Year Book Publishers, 35 East Wacker Dr., Chicago, IL 60601. Call 800-621-9262. ISBN 0-8151-5810-6, $15.95.

Choices and Consequences: What to Do When a Teenager Uses Alcohol/Drugs,[4] Dick Schaefer, 1987, 155 pages. Teaches parents how to recognize and intervene in teenage chemical dependency, clearly describes different approaches for teens verses adults. ISBN 0-935908-42-0, $9.95.

Parenting for Prevention, How to Raise a Child to Say No to Alcohol/Drugs,[4] David J. Wilmes, 1988, 135 pages. An excellent resource explaining enabling, eliminating it, and teaching lifeskills. ISBN 0-935908-46-3, $8.95.

Intervention: How to Help Someone Who Doesn't Want Help,[4,5] Vernon Johnson, 1986, 116 pages. Gives a plan for a caring and loving confrontation of the alcoholic with the goal of treatment. ISBN 0-935908-31-5, $8.95.

Not My Kid,[2] Beth Polson & Miller Newton, Ph.D., 1984, 224 pages. A parent's guide to prevention, recognition, and treatment of adolescent chemical use, especially strong on recognition of a problem with many personal stories. Avon Paperback Books, #69997-4, $2.95.

Toughlove:[1] Phyllis & David York and Ted Wachtel, 1982, 240 pages. The Yorks promote a workable, functioning family by refusing to use blame, sharing feelings as well as responsibilities, working within the family's financial resources, accountability for behavior, taking a stand and using the support of other parents. ISBN, 0-553-26783-3, Bantam Books, $4.50.

Raising Drug-Free Kids in a Drug-Filled World,[5] William Perkins & Nancy McMurtrie-Perkins, 1986, 96 pages. Written from personal experience on how to cope with kids before, during and after addictive drug use. ISBN 0-89486-316-9, $6.95.

What, When & How to Talk to Children about Alcohol and Other Drugs,[5] Gail Gleason Milgram, 1983, 87 pages. Especially good on communication skills between the generations. ISBN 0-89486-189-1, $5.95.

Let's Help Our Youth Choose Drug Free Lives,[6] Shelda Longerbeam and JoAnn Whitacre, 1984, 52 pages. A parent guide written by parents who founded a very successful parent group. $3.50, discounts for bulk orders.

Broken Heart - Whole Heart, Pecki Sherman & Virginia Newlin, 1987, 185 pages. A mother's story of her family's interactions and coping techniques during a long journey to find treatment for their drug-involved son. Hampshire Books, 1300 Weathervan Lane, #223, Akron, OH 44313, ISBN 1-877674-01-X, $9.95.

Codependent No More,[1,5] Melody Beattie, 1987, 208 pages. Ms. Beattie explains what codependency is, is not, who has it and how to move beyond it. ISBN 0-89486-402-5, $8.95.

Different Like Me, A Book for Teens Who Worry about Their Parents' Use of Alcohol/Drugs,[4] Evelyn Letite & Pamela Espeland, 1987, 120 pages. Gives teens a plan on how to live a fulfilling life when there is a parent who drinks too much. ISBN 0-935908-34-X, $6.95.

It Will Never Happen to Me,[5] Claudia Black, 1980, 183 pages. This book can lead to self-discovery and healing not only for the children of alcoholics, but for any children of families in serious trouble. ISBN 0-910233-00-9, $7.95.

Adult Children of Alcoholics,[5] Janet Woititz, 1983, 106 pages. The roles children in alcoholic homes take on is explained and how they can change. The children of "adult children" is another topic discussed. ISBN 0-932194-15-X, $6.95.

Under the Influence, A Guide to the Myths and Realities of Alcoholism,[1] James R. Milam and Katherine Ketcham, 1981, 237 pages. Gives new insights on the physiological aspects of alcoholism, treatment programs, and the role of nutrition in recovery. Bantam Books, Inc., ISBN 0-553-26758-2, $4.50.

Marijuana Alert,[2,3,7] Peggy Mann, 1985, 526 pages. A book about marijuana, the crisis, health hazards, and what is being done by parent groups, industry, and the government. ISBN 0-07-039906-9, $10.95.

The Sad Story of Mary Wanna or How Marijuana Harms You,[7] Peggy Mann, 1988. A 40 page booklet for grade school children to use individually, or as part of a school curriculum. $3.95. Teacher's Guide ($4.50) and Student Activity Book ($2.50) also available. Volume discounts available.

Keep off the Grass,[2,3] Gabriel G. Nahas, M.D., Ph.D., 259 pages. For teens and adults, a very distinguished scientist explains the effects of marijuana. $8.95.

800-Cocaine,[2,3,5] Mark S. Gold, M.D., 1984, 98 pages. Written by the founder of the 800-Cocaine Helpline, it tells all you need to know about cocaine and crack/cocaine. ISBN 0-553-34388-2, $3.50.

Schools Without Drugs, U.S. Department of Education, 1989, 87 pages. Covers the drugs, the disease, prevention, and the legal aspects of policy development, enforcement and search and seizure procedures for schools. ***FREE,*** Call 1-800-624-0100.

Drug Prevention Curricula, A Guide to Selection and Implementation, U.S. Department of Education, 1988, 65 pages. ***FREE,*** Call (301) 468-2600.

Enabling in the School Setting,[4] by Gary L. Anderson, 1988, 40 pages. Explains denial and enabling by school personnel and parents and how to stop it. ISBN 0-935908-43-9, $2.75.

Schools & Drugs, A Handbook for Parents and Educators,[8] Joyce M. Tobias, R.N., 1986, 30 pages. Handbook for parents and educators which describes alcohol and drug use in schools, what can be done about it and a program which has been initiated in a school system. ISBN 0-9616700-1-0, $3.00.

Courts & Drugs, A Court Watch Handbook for Citizens,[8] Patricia R. Smith, 1986, 30 pages. Handbook which contains all the information needed for monitoring (court watching) felony drug cases. It gives suggestions for setting up a Court Watch Program. Court procedures are described and an extensive glossary of legal terms is included. ISBN 0-9616700-2-9, $3.00.

Other Resources

Marijuana Alert: Slides from Scientists[7] - Slides show normal and pot-damaged cells, chromosomes, lung tissue, immune system cells, sperm, etc. A 40-minute audio cassette by Peggy Mann explains slides. $37.95 (31 Slides).

Marijuana: Myths and Misconceptions[2] - Appropriate for teens and adults, this 90-minute video by researcher, Dr. Robert Gilkeson, reviews the effects of drugs on the brain cells. It can be broken up into four 22-minute teaching sessions. Teacher's guide included. $400.

We Can Move the Mountains[6] - Video depicts how a community mobilized to deal with the problems of alcohol and other drugs and their harmful effects on young people, showing active participation from schools, treatment programs, law enforcement, civic organizations, churches, parents, and youth. $49.95 (20 minutes).

The Honor of All - Video which tells the true story of how an American Indian community decreased its alcoholism rate from 100% to 5%. Phil Lucas Productions, P.O. Box 1218, Issaquah, WA 98027, (206) 392-9482. (57 minutes)

Alco-Screen - A simple dip stick indicates the amount of alcohol in saliva by changing color. Can be used at home. Chem-Elec, Inc., P.O. Box 372, North Webster, IN 46555, (219) 834-4080, box of 25 sticks-$18.75.

The Rapid Eye Test to Detect Drug Influence, Forrest S. Tennant, M.D., Dr. P.H. Book instructs a parent or a professional to detect drug use by observing signs in the eye. Veract, Inc., 338 S. Glendora Ave., West Covina, CA 91790, 1-800-624-4540 or 1-800-821-0775 in California, $18.00.

Footnoted books and resources available from:

1. ***Book stores and public libraries***
2. ***Committees of Correspondence***: (617) 774-2641
3. ***Narcotics Education***: 1-800-548-8700
4. ***Johnson Institute***: 1-800-231-5165
5. ***Hazelden***: 800-328-9000
6. ***Kids Are Our Concern***: (703) 667-8365
7. ***Woodmere Press***: (212) 678-7839
8. ***PANDA PRESS***: Order form on page 126

FREE CATALOGUES

Offer many self-help, AA, Al-Anon and educational publications.

Hazelden: 800-328-9000
Johnson Institute: 1-800-231-5165
Narcotics Education: 1-800-548-8700
Community Intervention: 1-800-328-0417

COMMUNITY ACTION RESOURCES

Parents' Resource Institute for Drug Education, Inc. (PRIDE): National resource, information, center; offers consultant services to parent groups, school personnel, and youth groups; and offers a drug use survey service. Conducts an annual international conference. Publishes a newsletter, youth group handbook, and many other publications. Sells and/or rents books, films, videos, slide-shows, etc. Membership, $20.00. Write to PRIDE, the Hurt Building, Suite 210, 50 Hurt Plaza, Atlanta, GA 30303, 1-800-241-7946.

Committees of Correspondence, Inc.: Publishes informative newsletter and emergency news flashes on issues which need letters from the public. Sells excellent resource manual ($18.00), books, pamphlets and videos. Membership, $20.00. Write to CC, 57 Conant St., Rm. 113, Danvers MA 01923, (617) 774-2641.

Families in Action: Maintains a drug information center with over 100,000 documents. Publishes Drug Abuse Update, a 24-page newsletter containing abstracts of articles published in medical and academic journals and newspapers throughout the country; $25.00/4 issues. Write to FIA, 2296 Henderson Mill Rd., Suite 204, Atlanta, GA 30345, (404) 934-6364.

National Federation of Parents for Drug-Free Youth (NFP): A national "umbrella organization" which assists in the formation and networking of parent groups in every state. Offers workshops and a Training Manual for Drug-Free Youth Groups. Membership: youth, $10.00, adult, $15.00; group, $100.00. Write to NFP, 1423 N. Jefferson, Springfield, MO 65802, 1-800-7333-NFP.

TOUGHLOVE: Free self-help program and crisis-intervention program, which has structured group meetings to support parents and spouses in demanding responsible cooperation from out-of-control family members. This non-profit organization was founded by Phyllis and David York, certified drug and alcohol counselors, who developed the TOUGHLOVE program after experiencing out-of-control children in their own family. There are over 1500 groups. Training workshops and seminars are conducted throughout the country. TOUGHLOVE publishes a newsletter, books and a "how to" manual for starting a group. Write to TOUGHLOVE, P.O. Box 1069, Doylestown, PA 18909, (215) 348-7090.

Youth to Youth: National alcohol- and drug-free youth group which sponsors workshops and conferences across the country for kids and adults. Write to YTY, 700 Bryden Rd., Columbus, OH 43215, (614) 224-4506.

Campuses without Drugs: Campus chapters create a visible gathering place on campus for anti-drug activities. Offers drug education materials, speakers bureau, and newsletter. Membership: student, $10.00; adults, $20.00. Write to CWC, 2530 Holly Dr., Pittsburgh, PA 15235, (412) 731-8019.

U.S. National Clearinghouse for Alcohol and Drug Information: Request to be put on mailing list for new publications listings. Single copies free; parent groups may get free materials for distribution. Supplies and other assistance also available from your NCADI sponsored State RADAR Network. Contact NCADI for your RADAR location, P.O. Box 2345, Rockville, MD. 20852, (301) 468-2600.

SCHOOL RESOURCES

Private Organizations

These organizations offer consultation services, surveys, workshops, seminars, manuals, books, literature and films etc. for programs in schools, athletics, businesses and communities:

American Council on Drug Education (ACDE), 204 Monroe St., Rockville, MD 20850, (301) 294-0600.

Narcotics Education, Inc., 12501 Old Columbia Pike, Silver Spring, MD, 20904, 1-800-548-8700.

Hazelden Continuing Education Center, Box 11, Center City, MN 55012, 1-800-822-0080.

Johnson Institute, Inc., 7151 Metro Blvd., Minneapolis, MN 55435, 1-800-231-5165, (in Minnesota - 1-800-247-0484).

Community Intervention, Inc., 529 South 7th St., Suite 570, Minneapolis, MN 55415, 1-800-328-0417, (in Minnesota 612-332-6537).

National Association for Children of Alcoholics (NACoA), 31582 Coast Highway, Suite B, South Laguna, CA 92677, (714) 499-3889.

U.S. Department of Education Resources

The following five centers (1) train school personnel; (2) assist state education agencies in coordinating and strengthening local programs; (3) assist local agencies and post secondary institutions in developing training programs; (4) evaluate and disseminate information on successful prevention programs:

Northeast Regional Center
Super Teams, Ltd.
12 Overton Ave.
Sayville, NY 11782
(516) 589-7022

Includes Connecticut, Delaware, Maine, Maryland, Massachusetts, New Hampshire, New Jersey, New York, Ohio, Pennsylvania, Rhode Island, Vermont.

Southeast Regional Center
PRIDE, Inc.
Hurt Building, Suite 210
50 Hurt Plaza
Atlanta, GA 30303
(404) 688-9227

Includes Alabama, District of Columbia, Florida, Georgia, Kentucky, North Carolina, Puerto Rico, South Carolina, Tennessee, Virginia, Virgin Islands, West Virginia.

Midwest Regional Center
BRASS Foundation
2 North Riverside Plaza, No. 821
Chicago, IL 60606
(312) 324-9500

Includes Indiana, Illinois, Iowa, Michigan, Minnesota, Missouri, Nebraska, North Dakota, South Dakota, Wisconsin.

Southwest Regional Center
University of Oklahoma
555 Constitution Avenue
Norman, OK 73037
(405) 325-1711

Includes Arizona, Arkansas, Colorado, Kansas, Louisiana, Mississippi, New Mexico, Oklahoma, Texas, Utah.

Western Regional Center
N.W. Regional Education Lab
101 S.W. Main St., Suite 500
Portland, OR 97204
(503) 275-9500

Includes Alaska, American Samoa, California, Guam, Hawaii, Idaho, Montana, Nevada, Northern Marianas, Oregon, Trust Territory of the Pacific Islands, Washington, Wyoming.

Schools Without Drugs: The Challenge - A network for schools.
400 Maryland Ave. S.W.
Washington, D.C. 20202
(202) 357-6265

Network of Colleges and Universities Committed to the Elimination of Drug and Alcohol Abuse:
U.S. Department of Education
Washington, D.C. 20208-5644
(202) 357-6265

TWELVE STEP PROGRAMS

The 12 step programs are based on the 12 steps of personal change and the 12 traditions. They are free self-help groups which follow rules of strict anonymity. Members know each other only on a first name basis unless they choose to reveal their last name. The first 12 step program was Alcoholics Anonymous (AA), founded in 1935 for those who had problems with alcohol use. A separate fellowship, the Al-Anon Family Groups (AFG), formed after family members and friends of AA members began to attend AA meetings and discovered that when they applied the 12 steps to themselves, their own lives became more manageable and often sobriety was enhanced for their loved one. Alateen was formed to meet the needs of teenagers, and recently some adult groups have chosen a special focus, the "adult children of alcoholics" (AFG Adult Children). Practice of the program also enhances the lives of those associated with an ***active*** alcoholic, and often the alcoholic desires sobriety after those around him achieve serenity. Any drug user who also uses alcohol may attend AA, and the family and friends may attend Al-Anon. The other twelve step programs listed below are for users of any mind-altering substance and their family and friends. Each group publishes excellent literature, much of which is distributed free at meetings. The twelve step program has proven to be the most successful basis for professional treatment programs for users and their family and friends.

National Headquarters of Twelve Step Programs

For Family & Friends

Al-Anon World Service Office
P.O. Box 862, Midtown Station
New York, NY 10018-0862
1-800-344-2666/(212) 302-7240

Nar-Anon Family Groups
P.O. Box 2562
Palos Verdes Peninsula, CA 90274
(213) 547-5800

Families Anonymous, Inc.
P.O. Box 528,
Van Nuys, CA 91408
(818) 989-7841

For the User

Alcoholics Anonymous
World Services, Inc.
Box 459, Grand Central Station
New York, NY 10163
(212) 686-1100

Narcotics Anonymous
World Services, Inc.
P.O. Box 9999
Van Nuys, CA 91409
(818) 780-3951

There is no elevator to serenity; it requires twelve steps.

EVALUATION OF DRUG LITERATURE

Terminology Recommended by the U.S. Office of Substance Abuse Prevention (OSAP)

Watch for these terms in literature being evaluated.

1. "Mood-altering drugs" is a mild and inaccurate description of the powerful effect that drugs have on the mind. The phrase, "mind-altering," is preferred.

2. To emphasize that alcohol is a drug it is suggested that the phrase "alcohol and other drugs" be used instead of "substance abuse." Thus, it is stressed that alcohol should also be recognized as a drug.

3. Since all illicit drugs are harmful, drugs should not be referred to as "hard, soft, good, or bad" drugs. All drugs can and do cause damage to consumers.

4. "Use" is being used more in place of "abuse." This phrase includes the problems that result from any alcohol and other drug use, as well as excessive use. There is no "recreational" or "responsible" use of illicit drugs and we should refer to "drug use" for what it is.

5. Alcohol and other drug use does not result in traffic "accidents," it results in "crashes." The term "accident" refers to a consequence that could not have been avoided.

Research References

Material should include research references from the 1980's. Health consequences of use should be clear. The increased potency of today's marijuana and the devastating effects of cocaine need emphasis.

Pro-drug Literature

Much pro-drug literature is written by college professors who are members of pro-drug organizations, such as NORML, The National Organization for the Reform of Marijuana Laws. Organizations whose literature should be carefully scrutinized include Do It Now Foundation, Up Front, Wisconsin Clearinghouse, and Minnesota Prevention Resource Center. The literature will often overemphasize the harmfulness of alcohol, nicotine and caffeine, but play down the effects of other drugs, and talk about how to use other drugs safely, recreationally, responsibly or in moderation.

TV NETWORKS

NBC-TV Audience Services
30 Rockefeller Plaza
New York, NY 10020

ABC-TV Audience Information
1330 Avenue of the Americas
New York, NY 10019

CBS-TV Audience Services
51 West 52nd St., New York, NY 10019

LETTER WRITING TIPS

It has been estimated that one letter or call represents the opinion of 400 citizens. Citizen pressure can have a tremendous influence on elected officials, the media, and the products produced and advertised by businesses. Following are tips for writing to your congressman which can also be applied to other letter writing.

For quick or urgent communication Western Union offers several 24-hour services: mailgrams, personal opinion messages, and telegrams. Call 1 800-325-6000.

Address Letters to Congressmen:

Honorable__________________
United States Senate
Washington, D.C. 20510

Dear Senator________________

◆◆◆◆◆

Honorable__________________
House of Representatives
Washington, D.C. 20515

Dear Mr. or Ms.______________

One Subject per Letter: Confine each letter to one subject. ***do not*** indulge in long letters on many subjects.

Timeliness: A letter at a time when Congress is considering a particular measure is best.

Identify Yourself as a Constituent: Identify organizations to whom you are reporting.

Know Your Subject: Inform your Congressman why you support or oppose a piece of legislation. Identify the legislation by bill number (H.R.______ or S._____) or by name if it is widely publicized by a particular title. If you have expert knowledge on a subject, explain briefly your background in it. Support your position with facts, not generalities. Enclose clippings from the local newspaper, as appropriate. Be sure to name the newspaper and date. Often it is helpful to ask, "Will you support Bill #_______?"

Be Friendly: Letters from thoughtful friends or undecided voters have more influence than a letter from enemies or nagging critics. Don't berate your congressman.

Be Constructive: If you believe the bill is the wrong approach, explain another approach or offer suggestions for amendments.

Ask for a Reply: If you receive a noncommittal response, write again and ask for more details.

Urge Others to Write: Urge your family and friends to write on the subject.

No Form Letter! No Petitions! A sincere, well-thought-out letter from you is much more effective than a form letter or a signature on a petition.

A Pat on the Back: When your member of Congress votes "right," send a thank you note.

SUGGESTED GUIDELINES FOR PARENTS

AT HOME

Curfews

Grades 1-8: Home after supper

High School:

School days: Home after supper, except for special events.
Weekends: 11 p.m. to 12:30 a.m. depending on age, child, and events.
Vacation: 10:30 p.m. weekdays

Reasonable Rules

Telephone: A time limit on calls, no phones in children's bedroom, no private telephone lines for children.

Car: Require child to pay for insurance, gas, repairs, etc. Car keys will be taken away and license revoked if there is any chemical use.

Parents' Responsibilities

Know who children are going out with, their destination and a number where they can be reached.

Call the host of party to check that it will be supervised by an adult and no alcohol or drugs will be allowed.

Have an understanding with child that he/she may call parents for a ride home if child is in a situation where the driver has been drinking or doing drugs. If parents drink on evening child goes out it is best to make transportation arrangements for the child in case a ride is needed.

When child arrives home be up and have a conversation with him/her.

Know the parents of children's friends.

AT SCHOOL

Parents should know the school rules, expect their children to obey them, and support school personnel in their enforcement.

HOSTING PARTIES

Ground Rules

Set a time limit.
Invitation only, keep it small.
No smoking, alcohol or drugs.
No leaving premises and returning.
No gate crashers.
Lights should be left on.
Confine party to certain rooms.

Parents' Responsibilities

Parents are legally responsible for minors consuming alcohol or drugs in their home.

Be visible and available.

Welcome calls or visits from parents.

PARENT PLEDGE

I pledge that all parties in my home for school-age children will be chaperoned and will be free of alcohol and drugs.

Name ______________________________ Date __________

Name ______________________________ Date __________

School ________________________ Phone ______________

My phone number may be given to a parent who is inquiring about a party.

yes______ no______ Mail to: ______________

Pledge signers names will be kept on file. ______________

____

Call ______________ to check if the host of the party your child is invited to has signed the pledge.

LOCATING RUNAWAYS

1. Call parents of child's friends. Parents are sometimes harboring runaways and are not aware of it. Ask them if they have noticed anything unusual at their home, such as food missing, evidence of another person in the basement, garage, tool shed, etc. Offer a reward to child's friends for information. Keep a notebook and pencil near phone and record and date any conversations that may give the smallest bit of relevant information.

2. File a missing persons report immediately with the local police or sheriff, and ask them to file a report with the State Department of Justice or State Bureau of Investigation, and the National Crime Information Center (NCIC). Check if child is being detained for a crime anywhere. Stay in touch with authorities and follow up persistently.

3. Make a poster with photo, description, date of disappearance, any identifying marks, clothing or mannerisms and a contact telephone number (usually police) and address. Offer reward for verified information. Post in convenience stores, churches, and locations the child has frequented. Offer a reward in the newspaper. Try to get as much publicity as you can.

4. Check past telephone and credit card bills for out-of-town calls and purchases, job placement agencies and armed forces.

5. Consider employing a competent, carefully selected detective. Verify his character with the Better Business Bureau, and make your financial arrangements in advance with conditions spelled out in writing.

RUNAWAY AND PARENT SERVICES

Runaway Hotline: 1-800-231-6946, 1-800-621-4000 (24 hr.). Arranges confidential relay of messages from youths to parents without revealing locations. Provides shelter, counseling, medical, legal, and transportation referral services.

National Center for Missing and Exploited Children: 1-800-843-5678 (24 hr.). Information and referral geared to parents to locate missing children.

Child Find of America: 1-800-I-AM-LOST. For children who want to be reunited with their parents.

Salvation Army Missing Persons: (202) 783-4050, 503 E St. N.W., Washington, D.C. 20001. For immediate family members only; $5.00 filing fee.

NATIONAL HOTLINES

1-800-241-7946 - Pride Info. Line
1-800-COCAINE - Cocaine Hotline
1-800-662-HELP - NIDA
1-800-ALCOHOL - Alcohol Hotline
1-800 BAD-WEED - Report marijuana growing

PANDAA PHILOSOPHIES

Our children have the right to grow up in a drug-free environment. Parents have the responsibility to be informed about substance abuse, to communicate to their children a clear and firm "no use" position about alcohol and drug use, to set an example to their children, and to use consistent discipline combined with love and care.

A parent's responsibility takes precedence over a child's right to privacy whenever a situation is threatening to the child's health and safety.

PANDAA believes the use and abuse of both legal and illegal drugs has reached epidemic proportions. It has extended into every segment of our communities bringing with it corruption, violence, property loss, family disintegration and disregard for the law. It has become the number one health problem for the 15 to 24 year age group, the only age group with a rising death rate.

PANDAA opposes the use of illegal drugs or illegal use of mind-altering prescription drugs. PANDAA considers any alcohol use under the legal drinking age abuse. We consider ***alcohol to be a drug*** which affects emotional and physical development in adolescents, and is capable of producing dangerous changes in behavior and well-being.

The initiation of adolescent alcohol and/or drug use is caused by pro-alcohol and -drug media messages, drug using role models, peer pressure, curiosity, availability, acceptance by society, inadequate laws and enforcement of laws. Usage continues because it gives short term pleasure, it becomes a temporary problem solving tool, and society imposes few consequences for abuse. As usage continues it can develop into the disease of chemical dependency which affects the entire family and usually requires treatment. Adolescents can become dependent on alcohol or drugs in six months to one year. Dependency in the adult usually develops after a matter of years.

The use of drugs is a clear choice and the user is responsible for any actions committed while under the influence of any drug. Juveniles and adults involved in alcohol and drug related crimes should be evaluated for chemical dependency and where appropriate, treatment should be mandated, along with other appropriate consequences. We consider drug trafficking a violent crime requiring severe consequences.

The treatment of chemical dependency has a low success rate. Development of more successful treatment modes is needed. Treatment programs must be free of all mind-altering drugs including alcohol, and promote an alcohol and drug free-life style. Treatment programs should be accessible, affordable, and covered by health insurance plans.

Schools have an obligation to the community and the families they serve to provide an alcohol- and drug-free learning environment for students. Schools should provide drug education, strictly enforced consequences for violations, substance abuse recognition training for school personnel, help families recognize chemical dependency, and require treatment for readmittance to school when chemical dependency has been diagnosed.

Elected and appointed officials have a responsibility to be informed, enforce the laws as written, and support improved and necessary new laws.

★★★★★★★★★★★★★

ADDICT'S PRAYER

Father God,
We come before You today
In the name of all Your confused children,
For whom alcohol and drugs
Have become false gods.
We ask that through Your love
They may gain release
And find their way
To wholesome living.
We bow our heads in humility,
Mindful that each of us
Knows the snare
Of a destructive habit,
Whether it be
Food or tobacco or gossip,
Gambling or grudge-holding,
Ambition or greed.
Lord, let us see ourselves
Not separate from those we call addicts,
But comrades in a common struggle,
Bearing one another's burdens,
Sharing faith and courage,
On our imperfect journey
Toward Your perfect eternity.

Author Unknown

INDEX

Order Form for Books & PANDAA Newsletter

KIDS & DRUGS by Joyce M. Tobias, R.N. A 126 page handbook for parents and professionals that includes the drug culture, stages of chemical use, treatment, alcohol and other mind-altering drugs, prevention, and formation of parent groups.

SCHOOLS & DRUGS by Joyce M. Tobias, R.N. A 30 page handbook for parents and educators which describes alcohol and drug use in schools, what can be done about it, and programs and regulations which have been initiated in a school system.

COURTS & DRUGS by Patricia R. Smith. A 30 page handbook which contains all the information needed for monitoring (court watching) felony drug cases. It gives suggestions for setting up a Court Watch Program, describes court procedures, and has an extensive glossary of legal terms.

PANDAA Newsletter - 12 page educational newsletter published 4 time a year.

KIDS & DRUGS
Single copy . . . 6.00 each
2 to 9 copies . . . 5.50 each
10 to 49 copies . . 5.00 each
50 to 99 copies . . 4.00 each
100 to 499 copies . 3.00 each
500 or more . . . 2.00 each

SCHOOLS & DRUGS/COURTS & DRUGS
1 to 9 copies . . . . . . 3.00 each
10 to 24 copies . . . . . 2.00 each
25 or more copies . . . . 1.00 each

One copy of each book . . 10.00/set
PANDAA Newsletter . . . 7.00/yr.

NO.	ITEM	TOTAL
	Subtotal	
	Virginia residents sales tax 4.5%	
	Shipping: 15% of subtotal, 5% for orders over $50.00	
	PANDAA Newsletter	
	TOTAL	$

❐ Please send a free copy of the PANDAA newsletter to the enclosed names.

NAME____________________ PHONE__________

ADDRESS______________________________

CITY____________________ STATE______ ZIP__________

Please make checks payable to **Panda Press**. Mail order with check to **Panda Press**, 4111 Watkins Trail, Annandale, VA 22003. Phone (703) 750-9285.